THERE IS NO

The World vs. The Kingdom of God

Wisdom for Teens Powerful Enough for Adults

To Dalcina

love you, Be blessed

Thank you for your

Support

By Eric Brown

There Is No Comparison

The World vs. The Kingdom of God

Wisdom for Teens Powerful Enough for Adults

BY ERIC BROWN

Angel's Music

Detroit, Michigan

Unless otherwise indicated, all Scripture quotations are taken from the King James Version of the Bible.

There is No Comparison
ISBN 978-0-9832756-0-2
Copyright 1-545519991 2011
by Eric Brown
Angel's Music
P.O. Box 13385
Detroit, Michigan 48213

Published by Angel's Music, Inc. (*Publishing Department*)
Angel's Music
P.O. Box 13385
Detroit, Michigan 48213

Letter from the author to you,

I want to start by saying thank you for purchasing my first book, There is No Comparison. I'm grateful and hopeful that your life will be enriched by your purchase which means more to me than any money I receive for each book I sell. My journey in life has brought me to many different places in life and has taught me many things. One thing I have learned on my journey that I know is true is that it is better to give than to receive. Therefore, I give thanks to my God for my journey which has brought me to you so that I can give to you what I have freely received from Him. I bless you and I hope this book inspires you to live a life in freedom and in victory.

Sincerely yours,

E.L. Brown

Thank You

I thank you Father for your love, grace, and kindness that you have shown me consistently. Without you, there is absolutely no way that this book would have ever been finished and I want you to know personally that I am grateful and overwhelmed by your love. I thank you Pastor, Apostle Donald Coleman and First Lady Shay for your determination to see God's will fulfilled in your lives and the lives of others. I thank you Mother, Elsie Brown for your support and always being there for me no matter what I am going through; I have found that you are always there and I'm grateful, thank you. I want to thank all of the leaders at New Breakthrough Church international along with every member for being committed to fulfilling God's will. I want to thank my editors for doing a great job editing my book, Ms. Hicks and Akia Walton. I want to thank my good friend, Norman Plant, for helping me design my book cover and logo for my company. I want to thank the body of Christ as a whole, my family and my friends for your prayers, support and for the love you have shown me. I am grateful, love you all.

TABLE OF CONTENTS

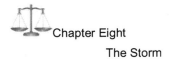Chapter Eight

The Storm

Chapter Nine

God's Love

Introduction

There Is No Comparison

When you look at this world and everything it has to offer—expensive clothes, costly jewelry, fancy cars, exquisite houses, beautiful women, handsome men, high-paying jobs, celebrity and fame, scary power, outrageous parties, explicit music and all its money and "bling"—you think: *"THAT'S* WHAT'S UP, *THAT* IS THE LIFE!

On the other hand, when you look at the Kingdom of God and all that God has to offer—peace, joy, truth, health, favor, abundance, purpose, meaning, destiny, and all His love—you think: "I CAN LIVE WITHOUT IT!" What you do not realize is that in reality, *"THAT* IS WHAT'S UP, *THAT* IS THE LIFE!" God's family is the only family on earth without lack, full of abundance, overflowing with resources, all-powerful, and unbeatable.

Throughout this book I call God's family **the Kingdom of God.** It is identified as a kingdom in which God is the King whose throne is in Heaven and who has sent His children to earth to rule over the whole earth. He has commanded them to be fruitful in the earth, to multiply in the earth, and to replenish and subdue the earth. The whole earth is God's: He created it; He formed it; and He filled it, but He has allowed His children to occupy the throne on the earth.

They will rule on the earth as partakers with Jesus who share His throne and authority forever (Revelation 3:21).

Throughout this book, I call Satan's family **the World** (which includes all individuals who refuse to repent and receive Jesus as Lord). The World is identified as a kingdom in which Satan is the King who has no power, no authority, and no dominion on the earth. He is very clever and cunning and his cleverness has allowed him to deceive many in the world into following after him. He has persuaded people to believe that his ways are the way to life, fun, riches, fame, and power, though in fact they are the way to destruction and eternal damnation. All of Satan's children lack in many areas of their lives. Not one of his children are wealthy—spiritually wealthy (which is the only wealth that really matters)—not one of them. They are all in poverty—spiritual poverty— which means *there is no life in them*. They have a joy poverty, meaning they have no joy. They have love poverty, meaning they never experience love because God is Love and they do not know God. Last but not least, they are in financial poverty because, even if they have a lot of money, their money is cursed by God and is theirs only temporary because it is laid up for the just, God's family (Proverbs 13:22).

This world's platform begins to lower as you obtain more wisdom and experience in your life. Proverbs 4:7 in the Word of God says *Wisdom is the principal thing; therefore get wisdom: and with all thy getting get understanding (KJV)*. You see, as most people get older they tend to realize that the world is full of lies, deceitfulness, and deadly poison. Though they gain wisdom through the things they experience in the world and discover that the ways of the world are corrupted, many people cannot turn from them because they do not understand that the only way to escape is to turn to God and His ways. Finally, there are only two kingdoms on the earth— *the Kingdom of God* and *the World*. Every individual belongs to one or the other.

Chapter 1

My Own Experience

Before I entered the Kingdom of God, I had no idea that up to that point in my life, everything I did was meaningless. All of my accomplishments meant nothing; all of the cars I had, all the fancy clothes I wore, all the expensive jewelry I wore, all the girls I dated, all the people I knew and all the respect I was given was worthless. My life had no purpose or meaning and it was filled with disappointments. I was just living the way I was taught and following the world's way of doing things, like the majority of people I knew.

The World had me trapped in a system that taught me how to think and what to value. It was almost as if I was brainwashed to go along with everything everybody else said and did. My dreams had become their dreams: to go to the NBA, to sell drugs and to become a rapper. My hopes had become their hopes: to get rich fast, become famous and be a big player. My thoughts had become their thoughts: self-driven, cunning and wicked. I was in over my head and the World had me just where they wanted me, trapped.

I had been tricked, fooled, misled, cheated, lied to, abused, taken advantage of and stripped of my own identity. I had become the World and the World was me. We were all one big unhappy family, doomed for everlasting hell fire and Satan (the prince of this world) was our father. It's one thing to know that your life is going in the wrong direction. However, it is a sad thing to know it and not be able to change and go in the right direction (Proverbs 3:5). Although I knew that my life was not right and that I wasn't who I pretended to be, I wasn't sure if I even wanted to change and go into the right direction. I just knew deep down inside that I was not the person I made known to everyone else.

Looking back, all I can say is what was I thinking or was I even thinking at all. Now it seems foolish for me to have followed people who were in a place in their life that they didn't want to be: always complaining, bitter, lacking peace, broke, stubborn, jealous, full of pride, disobedient, lacking their own identity and driven by twisted desires. There was no way that I could see. I had to be blind. Not to mention, I was living in the so-called lime light which could have been blinding me!

In the World's eyes, I was living the life! From my childhood on up, I never lacked much. I had the girls, the cars, the popularity, the game on and off the basketball court, the looks and the gear. I was cool! The girls loved me, the guys respected me and my old neighborhood was counting on me to be one of the first ones to make it out of the hood into a rich neighborhood. I really liked who I thought I was and the life I thought I was living.

As a kid, I played baseball, football and basketball, but basketball was my favorite; I loved to play some ball. If it snowed, I would shovel the snow up. If it rained, I would put on a rain coat and if it was hot, I would take my shirt off to play basketball. No matter how the weather was, I was determined to play basketball. I played basketball in elementary school, middle school and high school. I played basketball more than I did almost anything else growing up, which kept me out of a lot of trouble.

I never considered myself as a thug in my younger years. Although when I got older, I hung around some people who actually took people's lives and were involved with some big time drug dealers at one point. Sometimes I drove in cars with AK's in the trunk and pistols under the seat. But for the neighborhood I grew up in, this was nothing bad at all; it was normal for us. Drive-by shootings, selling drugs and people getting robbed was not out of the ordinary at all.

It was what I saw and what I heard growing up that made me the person I became. In the streets, at school and on TV, I saw the guy that everybody else looked up to, everybody admired, all the girls wanted and all the guys followed, and I wanted to be that guy. I was hearing that to be successful, you needed a lot of money, being a player was cool, to get high and drunk was what's up and to do what you wanted to do was it. I began to believe in what I saw and what I heard and that made me the way I was. I did whatever was necessary for me to do to become that guy. I bought the best clothes I could afford, best shoes, the hottest chains, the coolest watches, the sweetest rides. I had the nicest cut from my barber, James, in order to get the attention, the popularity, the girls, the fame and that name. Therefore, I did stuff just to be seen, just to be doing it and to be known. In high school, I was making scenes and acting wild everywhere I went so that I would be recognized so that people would be talking about me. Even on the basketball court, I would show off and try to make people fall and score thirty points on people. I would embarrass people and talk junk all through the game to let them know that they didn't have a chance at beating me or my team. So that when we got back home all my boys, D-Man, Tone, Rob & Larry would be telling everybody, "man Eric's cold; did you see how he made Marlowe fall on his face today?" What I wanted to be was not who I was; it was somebody else; an image *the World* made up for young men to follow in order to influence young men to be something other than who they really are.

When I was growing up around thirteen years old, I remember talking to my uncle Butch as he was sitting on my grandmother's porch. I was walking the basketball up and down the street dribbling between my legs. We were talking about girls and I remember him saying, "boy, you're still wet behind your ears, you haven't had none yet." I replied, "man whatever," wanting to be grown and pretending like I had already started having sex. But it was not much longer after that when I was around sixteen years old that I first had sex. The people I grew up around made sex seem like you had to have it or you would die. Now isn't that something, because you can have sex and catch a disease and die for real.

The truth is that it is better to wait 'til after you are married to have sex.

My mother was not home often because she worked long hours at an insurance company when I was growing up. So after school, I would normally go over to my grandmother's house to play with my cousins and wait until my mother would get off work. Then I would go home which was one house down from my grandmother's house. This is where my mother stayed with me and my little sister and brother, Carnita and Andre. Growing up was fun; however, I always desired to have a home where both of my parents were married and we all stayed together. My mother spoiled me so much that I was convinced growing up that there was nothing that I could not have. When I went to look for my first car, I was really upset because my mother would not buy me a brand new dodge Durango. I was in the 10th grade and I was literally talking back to my moms, cursing out loud and just out of control because I was so used to getting my way. I didn't know how to act when I didn't get my way. I was a momma's boy. My mother, Elsie, told me that she didn't remember me ever crawling because she would always have me in her arms. The next thing she knew, I was "on the floor running, not walking but running." I don't recall any time that my mother hit me, but I know she had to when I was younger at least once, but I don't remember it. However, I remember getting a whipping once by my grandmother, Emma, when my cousin Jamar convinced me to steal some G. I. Joe toys from the store with him. We both were caught, and when we made it home, my grandmother took out a belt and beat both of us. That was the first and last time I recall taking anything from a store growing up.

The one thing I wanted growing up and I did not have was a father figure that I could talk to. There were no older male figures in my life that I could look to and see or hear something other than what I had always seen and heard. There were no Apostle Coleman, Elder Sheards, Elder Brown, Elder Hughes or Elder Radolph (my Pastor and elders from my church) that I could turn to in order to see and hear something that wasn't said in the World or to encourage me in my journey of life. The men in my life growing up were scarce. I do not recall any of them really taking me by the hand to show me that there is more to life than what I had been living. I needed that, a father figure in my life to show me that he cared about the decisions I made, to encourage me and to speak blessings into my life. A father figure would have caused me to be a better person and that would have pushed me to give my best in life in everything I did. I know my mother cared and my family cared, but I really needed a father figure with a loving and humble spirit to show me something other than what I had saw and heard, both by his example and by speaking good things about me. I remember playing basketball for Denby High School, and I wanted my Dad to come and see me play, but I don't ever recall him coming to any of my games. It means the world for a young man to see his father sitting and watching him play ball in the stands. It means a lot to hear him cheering and saying, "number 15, that's my son." I never had that. I needed that and I believe every young man needs that. It is important for someone to show him that they are interested in his life and that he cares about the decisions that he makes, someone to encourage him and not put him down, someone to open up to them and love them for who they are. I never really talk much about my childhood because much of it, I don't remember, and it is mainly because that part of my life was missing. That man to be there for me when I needed him, that man that I knew cared, and that man that encouraged me and I knew loved me for me.

Two weeks before high school graduation, my daddy died. We didn't have the closest relationship, although he did come around on my birthdays and on Christmas to bring me gifts and to see my family. For some reason, I would act really good when he came around and I showed him a lot of respect, even more than my mother. I used to think that it was cool to talk back to my mom and to curse and swear in front of her, I don't ever recall cursing at my mother but I had a bad habit of talking back to her and cursing in front of her. While I was at my father's funeral, tears begin to flow vigorously down my face, not because of my feelings for him although he was my dad, but because in my mind, all I could think of was this question, Who Is Going To Be My Father Now? I desired something I never thought I really had and I felt that a father would be needed in my life for me to take the next step to become a man.

To think back, it's amazing, my earthly father told everybody I was not his son and even took my mother to court when I was younger, but my heavenly Father took me to court when I got older. Dropped all the accusations I had brought up against Him growing up by neglecting His words and being a disobedient son. Then He waited patiently for me to ask the question, "who is going to be my father now?" He was the first one to stand in heaven and say, "*Son, I will be your Father, for I have always been your Father even when you had not been a son.*" That's the picture I see when I think about how he saved me.

Now after graduating from high school, I went down south to play basketball for Alabama State University, but I never ended up playing. I was more interested at this point in chasing young pretty women. I spent three whole years down there before dropping out and didn't accomplish anything except meeting some really good people who I try to keep in contact with even today.

I left Alabama State and came back home and hooked up with some of my cousin's friends who were known as the Brick Boys in the nineties, some of Detroit's biggest drug dealers. Three months after we connected, we went to Vegas on a business trip that involved some drug trafficking, money laundering and I couldn't tell you what else. I was connected because somebody at all times needed to be with the two top dealers. They allowed me to be a part since I could be trusted, I was smart and I knew the streets. This was different from what I was used to; they really were connected and lived almost all of their life in the game.

Almost everything that I didn't see in the World while I was growing up in the hood and in school, I saw with them. From unloading semi- trucks of weed and cocaine in warehouses to driving the most expensive cars and even living in a mansion for short period of time in Vegas, I did it.

We were living the so-called life, I was twenty-two and I felt like Scar Face, "The World is all mine!" I would come home from Vegas to Detroit and drive downtown in an all white 500 Benz with 20 inch Lorenzo rims on it with a twenty thousand dollar kit, with cream leather interior, and looking better than a scrumptious box of chocolate, with a fresh hair cut, red gold chain around my neck and with diamonds in my techno watch. There wasn't too much anyone could tell me at this point. I was where I always wanted to be; ON TOP.

This all happened within an eight month period; all after I left from college at Alabama State in 2003. I get the impression that God wanted me to see the best this world had to offer me in order to be able to declare and proclaim that the life God has for you is far better, more abundant and it last much longer. I believe He wanted me to see that "There Is No Comparison between The World and His Kingdom."

I get the impression that God wanted me to see the best this world had to offer me in order to be able to declare and proclaim that the life God has for you is far better, more abundant and it last much longer.

On one hand, I started feeling disappointed with life as I traveled back down south to Alabama. On the other hand, I was excited because I was on my way back down south to shut the whole city down by showing off the new creamy pearl Lexus 430, with 20 inch rims. I'm telling you, it looked like a spaceship and I knew all my boys were going to be stunned and the girls would go crazy when they saw me driving a Lexus.

Somehow, the eleven hour trip from Detroit to Alabama took longer than I expected. I felt something very valuable was missing in my life and without it my life was useless, but I couldn't figure out what it was. <u>Can you imagine being in a place in this world where everybody else you know is trying to get and your soul begins to call out for something more. It even begins to scream out on the inside of you that there must be much more to life than this. That's something else isn't it</u>; okay let me get back to the story. When I arrived in Alabama, they reacted just like I thought; they went berserk.

I thought they would be happy to see me, but they were happy to see the car, the chain and the watch. When I drove on campus, everybody stopped what they were doing; all the girls in the dorms stuck their heads out of their windows and all eyes were on me. I thought I would love the attention, but on the second day there, it was too much for me to handle. I saw the hatred, jealousy and envy in most of the young men's eyes. I felt the intentions of the young women trying to find their way to survive. I was fed up with my life and the World.

I left Alabama State and as soon as I got home, I stopped by my cousin's friend's house. This was the guy who put me on and connected me with the rest of the crew. I then knew something was wrong; my mother had been calling my cousins a lot because she was really worried about me, seeing that I had not been home for months, and she was wondering where I was. Therefore, I ended up dropping the Lexus off at his apartment and going home for a while to my grandmother's house.

Now at my grandmother's house, my mother, my uncle, my brother and my sister all lived there with my grandmother. We all moved in together when I was in the eleventh grade on Bliss Street when my grandmother's house on Longview caught on fire. Nobody was hurt by the fire although my grandmother was in the house her dog Polo jumped on her bed and woke her up and she made it out of the house with the dog safe. Thank God, I loved my grandmother.

On Bliss, my grandmother, mother, uncle, brother and sister all stayed upstairs and I stayed in the basement. When I came back home from Alabama, I stayed in my old room in the basement. One night, I was in my room and it had to be close to midnight; I picked up a Bible that my mother bought me some years back for Christmas. I begin to read the book of Proverbs. What happened next is the reason my life has never been the same.

God spoke to me. Yes GOD spoke to me. He said, *YOU HAVE BEEN LIED TO; YOU HAVE BEEN TRICKED AND EVERYTHING THE WORLD HAS TOLD YOU HAS BEEN A LIE.* Then I went to sleep, and I woke up in the morning and confessed all of my sins and asked Jesus to come into my heart, and that is exactly what He did. I was completely changed. I told God everything that I did wrong that I could remember. I told Him about all my sins and even sins I planned on committing in the future. He forgave me, and from that day on, I was never the same.

In John 10:4 it reads, *And when he (Jesus) brings*

out his own sheep (His children), he (Jesus) goes before them; and the sheep (His children) follow him, for they (His children) know his voice (Nkjv).

God speaks to His children.

Jesus was sharing with His people that those who He has called, who have received Him as their Lord and Savior, that they hear from Him and they know His voice. When a unbeliever gives his life to Jesus and becomes a believer, Jesus comes to live on the inside of the believer and the believer is able to hear Him speak to him, to feel His presence as he prays to Him and is able to sense and experience His love. Jesus said in *Mathew 7:7* **Ask, and it shall be given you; seek, and ye shall find; knock, and it shall be opened unto you: For every one that asketh receiveth; and he that seeeeth findeth; and to him that knocketh it shall be opened (Kjv).** He was telling believers that as they <u>continue</u> to seek His face, they would eventually hear His voice, experience His presence, and His love.

The Key to hearing God's voice is to receive Jesus as Lord and continue to pursue God. He wants every believer to know Him personally.

To get back to the story, I went upstairs the next day and my mother looked at me and she said something that I didn't know exactly how to reply to. She asked me, "Who Are You?" She had seen the change that happen in me and saw that her prayers had finally been answered. I know now the answer to that question that my mother blurted out at me. I am a son of God. My Father sent Jesus to bring forth many sons, and now I am one of them.

Hebrews 2:10

For it became him **(Jesus),** *for whom are all things, and by whom are all things, in bringing many sons unto glory, to make the captain of their salvation perfect through sufferings (Kjv).*

From that day on, I never had sex again, I never went back to hanging with the big time drug dealers and I was finally free from the power of darkness and transformed into the Kingdom of God's dear Son. What is so amazing is that at the time, I did not have a job; I was no longer in school; I didn't know what to do next, but nothing mattered because the void that was in my heart had finally been filled with God's love. I had Jesus and He became my Lord and the Holy Spirit my guide. There was nothing in the world that I would trade for knowing Him, talking to Him, Him talking to me, embracing His love, and bringing people to Him.

John 3:16

For God so loved the world, that he gave his only begotten Son, that whosoever believeth in him should not perish, but have everlasting life (Kjv).

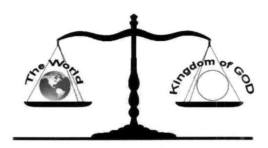

Chapter 2

Laying a Foundation

Mathew 4:23

And Jesus went about all Galilee, teaching in their synagogues, preaching the gospel of the kingdom, and healing all kinds of sickness and all kinds of disease among the people (Nkjv).

The Kingdom of God is what Jesus preached when He first began His ministry on the streets of Galilee. Then He found Peter, Andrew and John, and asked them to follow Him and they did. Then Jesus went through all Galilee teaching in their synagogues, preaching on their streets the Kingdom of God and healing all types of sickness and diseases among the people. Jesus became very famous because of the miracles He did. People brought Him many sick people that had all kinds of diseases, those which were tormented, those which were possessed with devils, those who were mentally ill and those who were paralyzed and He healed them all.

People came from all over to follow Him. Everybody wanted to meet Him; everybody wanted to know who He was, and everybody wanted to see the miracles that He did. Jesus was more popular than anyone during His ministry; however many rejected His message and neglected His reason for coming to the earth. Nevertheless, Jesus still continued to preach the good news of His Kingdom coming into the earth, to reveal to man His original purpose, His true identity, and His position in God's Kingdom as a son.

Man's original purpose was to please God. In Revelation 4:11 it says, *You are worthy, O Lord, to receive glory and honor and power; for you created all things, and by your will they exist and were created (Nkjv)*. Man was not created to live a selfish life or to seek after his own pleasure. He was created to please God. Jesus pleased God when He lived on the earth and God used Jesus to demonstrate to man how to please Him.

In John 8:29 Jesus said, *And he that sent me is with me: the Father hath not left me alone; for I do always those things that please him (Kjv)*.By doing this, Jesus revealed the desire and passion of sons in God's Kingdom. Their heart's desire and passion is to please their King. Each son that enters the Kingdom of God lays down his life as an act of love to please the King. Man's original purpose was also to look like, act like and rule like God Himself. In Genesis 1:26 it says,

And God said, Let us make man in our image, after our likeness: and let them have dominion over the fish of the sea, and over the fowl of the air, and over the cattle, and over all the earth, and over every creeping thing that creepeth upon the earth (Kjv).

The earth is the territory in the Kingdom of God that God gave to man to rule. The same way that He rules in heaven, He wanted man to rule on the earth. God's desire for man was that he would be His visible expression to His whole creation. His offspring that enforced His government everywhere he went. Jesus came to establish the Kingdom of God on the earth so that the Fathers desires were fulfilled.

The Holy Spirit spoke to me one day and He said: *Many people think of heaven and the kingdom of God as a place, but you must not think of it as a place but as a government that goes where ever its people go.* The Holy Spirit was revealing to me the truth about heaven and the Kingdom of God. It is here with us now. He wanted me to completely change the way I thought about heaven and the Kingdom of God as a place somewhere far away that I would go to when I died. He wanted me to realize the truth that the Kingdom of God is the reign and rule of God in any territory or land. Also, where ever the Kings children go His government follows. No matter where His children go, the Kingdom of God is established because the King's authority has been delegated to them.

The second thing Jesus came to do is to reveal to man

His true identity that could only be found in Him. Adam, the first man God created, sinned against God, and it brought forth death to his spirit, which caused him to lose the glory that God had given him along with his dominion. That glory was not just the beautiful glow that shined round about him from the Spirit of God. It was the very life of God. God's Word was in Adam and it was the only life he had.

God's word is the only life there is.

That glory was also the core of His opinions, judgments, and views. The word, Glory, in Hebrew is Kabod. It means weight, splendor, abundant in supply or quantity and glory. However, in the original Greek language, it shows a different side of glory. In Greek, the word, Glory, is translated Doxa, which means opinion, judgment and view. It also means, praise, honor, glory, splendor, brightness, majesty and the same kingly majesty which belongs to God as supreme.

When Adam lost the glory of God, his sight was changed. This happened to everyone else according to the Word of God, because we all were in Adam (Romans 5:18,19). So all of our sight was adjusted and we started to live according to what we perceived to be true instead of what God said was true. We started to live independent of God, even when we were created to be dependent on God. We picked up someone else's nature, a sinful nature of death when

Adam brought us into a relationship with Lucifer, the fallen Angel. He took our dominion over the earth when Adam and Eve disobeyed God and ate the fruit God told them not to (Genesis 3:6).

Lucifer had been kicked out of heaven by God because of pride that was found in his heart. Lucifer wanted to be like God and wanted to sit in the place that God was in. Therefore, God removed him completely from his position as the director of the choir in heaven, to no position at all (Isaiah 14:12-14). Other angels who agreed that Lucifer should sit in God's seat were kicked out of heaven as well.

Adam's disobedience to God also caused him and his wife Eve to forfeit their life. God told them that they could eat of the fruit of every tree in the garden, except the tree of the knowledge of good and evil or they would die (Gen. 2:16, 17). Eve, Adam's wife, was tricked by Satan and ate the fruit from the tree and gave some to Adam and he ate. Their disobedience killed them spiritually. Adam and Eve had access to all wisdom, understanding and knowledge through God. An example of this is when God told Adam to name the animals. Adam's ability to name every animal revealed Adam's connection to His Father who is Wisdom. This also gave Adam a correct opinion, judgment and view about everything, but after they ate the fruit, it cut off his relationship with God. Sin separated Adam from his Father and brought death to Adam and caused him to live, yet without LIFE for GOD is LIFE.

The third reason Jesus came was to position us as sons in His Kingdom. Therefore, Jesus had to come as the perfect sacrifice to lay down His life, that we might have life. He came to take us out of our old sinful body of Adam and to put us in His body, the Body of Christ. Through his sacrifice and obedience to God, He removed our disobedience and gave us the gift of righteousness that we could never earn by our own works (Romans 5:18, 19).

He came to take us out of our old sinful body of Adam and to put us in His body, the Body of Christ.

He revives our spirit and causes us to be back in the place Adam was before he fell. In the place of rest where we are not led by our souls, our minds or by Satan, but only by His Spirit in which we are led which assures us that we are sons of God. Romans 8:14 reads: **For as many as are led by the Spirit of God, they are the sons of God** *(Kjv)*. Jesus saved us from the power of sin and the dominion it had over us. Romans 6:16 says, **Know ye not, that to whom ye yield yourselves servants to obey, his servants ye are to whom ye obey; whether of sin unto death, or of obedience unto righteousness** *(Kjv)?*

Before this happens, we are deceived into believing lies that oppose the knowledge of God (2 Corinthians 10:5). The enemy blinds our minds in order to keep us from knowing the truth, which is Jesus Christ (2 Corinthians 4:4). These things keep us from entering into God's kingdom and our place as sons of God with dominion over the earth. From the place that makes the enemy subjected to us (Luke 10:19).

Furthermore, Jesus came to reveal to man what God intended for our earthly experience to be like. Imagine a life of unspeakable joy, peace that passes all understanding and an unconditional and unfailing love relationship with the creator of all things, Jesus Christ. This and more is what Jesus came to give man if he would repent, change his mind and turn from his sins to Him. Jesus came to show the world how much He loves, adores, and admires His creation by giving His life to establishing His kingdom on the earth for all men to enter.

Jesus came to show the world how much He loves, adores, and admires His creation by giving His life to establishing His kingdom on the earth for all men to enter.

Isaiah 9:6-7

For unto us a child is born, unto us a son is given: and the government shall be upon his shoulder: and his name shall be called Wonderful, Counselor, The mighty God, The everlasting Father, The Prince of Peace. Of the increase of his government and peace there shall be no end, upon the throne of David, and upon his kingdom, to order it, and to establish it with judgment and with justice from henceforth even for ever. The zeal of the LORD of hosts will perform this (Kjv).

Chapter 3

Can Anything Compare

Isaiah 40:18, 21-22

To who then will you compare to God? or what likeness will you compare unto him?... Have you not known? have you not heard? have it not been told you from the beginning? have you not understood from the foundations of the earth? It is he that sits upon the circle of the earth, and its inhabitants are like grasshoppers; who stretches out the heavens like a curtain, and spread them out as a tent to dwell in (Nkjv).

What can compare to God and His Kingdom? In Him are treasures not yet discovered, riches that money can't buy, wisdom for the old and young and pleasures beyond what we know forevermore. He is priceless to know and His Kingdom is to die for. The whole world belongs to him and everything in it. The Psalm of David beautifully sums up the King and His Kingdom in how His authority is delegated to His Son, mankind on the Earth.

Psalm 8:1-6O

Lord, Our Lord How excellent is Your name in all the earth, Who have set Your glory above the heavens! Out of the mouth of babes and nursing infants You have ordained strength, Because of Your enemies, That You may silence the enemy and the avenger. When I consider Your heavens, the work of Your fingers, The moon and the stars, which You have ordained, What is man that You are mindful of him, And the son of man that You visit him? For You have made Him a little lower than the angels, And You have crowned him with glory and honor. You have made him to have dominion over the works of Your hands; You have put all things under his feet (NKJV).

This Psalm describes how God crowned man with glory and honor, gave him complete dominion over the works of his hands and put all things under man's feet. He shows constant care and affection for man through His constant thoughts of him and through visiting him. This Psalm helps us to see what God's kingdom is all about and why nothing else can compare. The remarkable trust and unfailing love God the Father shares with His children is exemplified by giving them a huge role to play in His kingdom. He knows that through their relationship with one another, they will fulfill his agenda. However, there is a question that must be answered by YOU that Isaiah the prophet asked.

Who has believed our report (Kjv)? This is the question that Isaiah asked God in Isaiah 53:1. He wanted to know who on the Earth agreed with what God had said. He wanted to know if there was anybody out there that could hear or if there was anybody that could see. He knew that God was the only one able to open man's eye, and he knew that without God, no one would believe (1cor 2:11).

We often believe the words of man a lot easier than the Word of God because we have been trained and taught how to live by fear and not faith in this world's system. God is a God that cannot lie; if He said it, He is more than able to do it. We have also been taught to live a life dependent on ourselves and independent of God. That's why we <u>must learn</u> when God draws us into His Kingdom how to be dependent on Him, how to trust in Him, how to love Him and how to serve Him. This is because we have never served Him before; we have only served ourselves, others and the devil.

That's why the Word of God says, *Therefore if any man be in Christ he is a new creature: old things are passed away; behold, all things are become new* in 2 Corinthians 5:17 (Kjv). The only way for you to hear and understand what the Spirit of God is saying through the pages of this book is if He gives you an ear to hear and a heart to understand. The way to life and the way to truth are in Him alone. He is without beginning and without end and nothing else comes close to who He is.

Our position is that we have a choice to see things the same way the World sees things or begin to see things the way that He sees them. You have to question yourself: "Do I know more than God? Or, am I smarter than Him?" Life is in the very words He speaks. From the beginning of the creation, He spoke the sun into existence and today that sun still hangs in the sky by the power of the words He spoke back then. ***And God said let there be light: and there was light*** (Genesis 1:3, KJV). Furthermore, the only one who has the power to stop the sun from shining is Him.

God has always done things in such a way that is uncommon to man. He puts stars and a moon in the air to decorate the sky at night. He is brilliant. Some days, He even paints the sky gray and dark blue, even reddish at times. How can we understand His ways, His strategies or His plans or His love without Him. He is everywhere at the same time. There is nothing hidden from Him. Nothing happens without Him knowing that it is going to happen.

He is simply amazing in all His ways. He gives us the opportunity to cherish Him, to seek His face and the privilege to call on His name, Jesus the name above all names. He is excellent and His mercy endures forever. Everything consisted of Him, stands because of Him and comes from Him. Nothing that is created or that exist came from what we see with our natural eyes; it came from Him (Hebrews 11:3). He is the creator and maker of Heaven and Earth.

One day while I was in church, Evangelist Willis stood up and said that God had pressed upon her heart three things that He could not do. She said that He told her, "*I cannot lie, I cannot fail, and I cannot make you serve me.*" Soon after she stood up, I heard the voice of the Holy Spirit say to me, "*I have given man the power of choice and he chooses to obey Me or not to obey Me.*" These words were hard for me because I knew that many were choosing not to obey Him.

The words gripped my heart and I felt uneasy because of His love for us, the love that He shows me and the love that we share together. I knew that it was not easy for Him to say that knowing His love for man. But He made it up in His mind that He would let man decide to obey Him or disobey Him, to love Him back and live by His Word, or to hate Him and reject His Word. We have a choice and no matter what we choose, He will respect our decision. He is love and He wants us to choose to obey Him so that He can give us all that He has for us; however, if we disobey and choose otherwise, He is not going to make us change our decision. He will continue to chase after us though.

When we look at the choices we make on a regular basis, we see our future. Our future is not in days ahead of us, our future is today. How you spend your time today is how you are spending your future, by the choices you make today. We have the responsibility to choose wisely and our wise decision stems from the fear of the Lord.

Our future is not in days ahead of us, our future is today.

In Proverbs 1:7, it lets us know that, **the fear of the Lord is the beginning of knowledge: but fools despise wisdom and instruction** (Kjv). Our knowledge begins only at the point we reverence, honor and respect highly our Lord Jesus Christ. Out of our reverence for Him comes the guidance and leading that we were designed to follow that causes our lives to work out and our future to be bright. As we allow our light to shine, we live out the very purpose of our existence on the Earth. We have the privilege of letting the world see His beauty penetrate our vessels as we live in constant reverence of Him; realizing that He is the Kingdom, the power, the glory and nothing can compare to Him.

Out of our reverence for Him comes the guidance and leading that we were designed to follow that causes our lives to work out and our future to be bright.

Mark 4:30-32

He said, "To what shall we liken the kingdom of God? Or with what parable shall we picture it? It is like a mustard seed which, when it is sown on the ground, is smaller than all the seeds on earth; ³² but when it is sown, it grows up and becomes greater than all herbs, and shoots out large branches, so that the birds of the air may nest under its shade" (KJV).

Chapter 4
The Set Up (Words)

Mathew 12:36-37

But I say unto you, That every idle word that men shall speak, they shall give account thereof in the day of judgment. For by thy words thou shalt be justified, and by thy words thou shalt be condemned (Kjv).

Our words are the greatest and most powerful instruments used in the world today. By "The Word", God formed the world, and by our words we form our world. We must be wise in the words we choose to speak on a regular basis because our words identify us with the World or with the Kingdom of God. Jesus made it very clear to us how important it is to say the right thing. He said in Mathew 12:36-37 *But I say unto you, That every idle word that men shall speak, they shall give account thereof in the day of judgment. For by thy words thou shalt be justified, and by thy words thou shalt be condemned (Kjv).*

Our words identify us with The World or with the Kingdom of God.

Jesus is sharing His heart with His people. Jesus understood how the World made it seem like words didn't mean much at all and He wanted His people to know that your words mean more than you can imagine. That is why He stated that for every single word we speak, we must be prepared to give an answer to the reason why we said what we said. Just think for a moment, Jesus is revealing to you that every word that you say is being recorded. God has assigned angels to write down and record in books every single word you say. The reason why is not because God wants to condemn you, punish you or judge you, but because He desires a one on one personal relationship with you. The only way this can happen is when you believe what God has already said in His Word, agree to say what He said about you, about Himself and about this world.

Luke 12:32 says; *fear not, little flock; for it is your Father's good pleasure to give you the kingdom (Kjv).* God delights in giving gifts to His children. He loves to see them happy, prosperous, blessed and pleased in life. He knows all about us and He wants us to know all about Him. He wants to spend every second with us; talking, laughing and sharing His love with us. However, the words we speak can push Him away from us because they can reject His knowledge and agree with the knowledge of the World. This is not what God desires, but He will allow you to decide what you are going to speak. By doing so, you are deciding who you desire to spend your time with.

The words we speak can push God away from us because they can reject His knowledge and agree with the knowledge of the World.

When God first created man, He had a vision of what man would be like, how he would carry himself and what his position would be in His kingdom. His vision was that man would be just like Him. God wanted man to be so much like Him that the first time He mentions man He mentions Himself. In Genesis 1:26 He said *let US make man*, he didn't stop there, he goes on to say, *in OUR image*; you would think that He would be satisfied with that statement; however, He continued by saying *in OUR likeness*. The bottom line is that God wanted man to say what He says.

The bottom line is that God wanted man to say what He says.

Therefore, we must conclude that Satan, who is the

father of the World, wants his children to say what he says. This gives him the right to rule over them, to direct their path and to dominate their lives. It even helps him when people believe his words and speak what he says; because when man goes against what God has said, then there are certain things that man brings on himself because of what the word of God says. In Galatians 6:7-8 it reads; *Be not deceived; God is not mocked: for whatsoever a man soweth, that shall he also reap. For he that soweth to his flesh shall of the flesh reap corruption; but he that soweth to the Spirit shall of the Spirit reap life everlasting (Kjv).*

Whatever you choose to sow is what you are going to reap; your words are seeds, therefore, if you are sowing what Satan says, then you are going to reap bad things. If you sow what God says, you are going to reap good things and everlasting life. What you reap starts now, not later, and there is going to be evidence of what you have sowed by what you have said in your life. This evidence is going to be manifested by your lack of peace, joy, hope and love. Many people in the World think that these things are from bad luck or that they are just having a bad day, week or year. However, it is not bad luck or any of those things. You are just reaping what you have been sowing by saying the wrong things. This holds true when you say the right things. The evidence is always going to be better no matter what is going on in your life. You are going to have peace, joy, hope and be confident that you are going to make it even in the toughest times in your life. That is why the children of the Kingdom are always on top because they know that no matter what happens, if they say what the King says, everything is going to be okay.

You are just reaping what you have been sowing by saying the wrong things.

The World has taught us, especially in America, to say whatever we want, whenever we want and how ever we want. We have been trained to think that those things that are not normal, at all, are normal and okay. We see it on television, we hear it on the radio, we experience it in our schools and then we practice it every day for fun. However, we do not realize that the things that we think are cool and fun to say is shaping our world and causing bad things to come into our life and many good things to leave our life.

The words that we speak can bring us to a place of success in life, and it can bring us to a place of failure. Our words can also lift people up, and our words can tear people down. Our words reveal to us who we believe that we are, who we believe and trust in, what we think our purpose in life is and what family we belong to, **The World** or **The Kingdom of God**. Jesus said in Matthew 12:34 *for out of the abundance of the heart the mouth speaks (Nkjv)*. Have you ever heard the comment that some people make when they say or do something they should not have done or said. They say,

"God knows my heart." I do too; every word that you have said in the last 24 hours while I have been around you came from inside of it. *For as a man thinketh in his heart, so is he the word of God says in Proverbs 23:7 (Kjv).*

We are tempted by the words of people in many ways growing up, oftentimes by people Satan uses that are closest to us. These people never consider the effect the words that they speak over us can have on us; they are deceived. Many children have suffered terribly through the abuse of loved ones who have spoken harsh to them, put them down and called them names. You would think that the effects of words spoken to children growing up would leave them by the time they become adults; however, many have never been able to overcome the words that have been spoken over them as children. When family members told them they would not amount to anything, teachers told them they were stupid or a friend said they were ugly, these words were accepted and believed and they never recovered from the words these people spoke over their lives, even as adults.

Many people have learned behavior that comes from things that people have spoken over their life that they believe are true. They subconsciously act out those beliefs on a regular basis, not knowing why they act the way they do, based on thought patterns that have been formed over the years through the words of others. Most of the time, people don't even realize the lies that they have accepted, until they have been exposed to the truth. People struggle with relationships, have attitude problems, stress issues and have all kinds of things happen, even illnesses, because of misused words spoken over their life. Most of it is done in ignorance; however, the devil takes advantage of these words and uses them against them.

They subconsciously act out those beliefs on a regular basis, not knowing why they act the way they do, based on thought patterns that have been formed over the years through the words of others.

Every word we speak has an effect on nature, us and others. We all must realize the power that is in our tongues, the Bible says in Proverbs 18:21 **death and life are in the power of the tongue: and they that love it shall eat the fruit thereof** *(Kjv)*. Therefore, you can experience life through the words you say or you can experience death; it is all up to you. This is also true with the words others speak over you, they can make your life better by speaking good words, or they can make your life worse by speaking bad words.

The battle of the mind is what the children of God have to face in the renewing process when they enter into the Kingdom of God. The devil hates the fact that those individuals he once had control over and ruled now have separated from his kingdom, "The World," and now are saying and agreeing with what God says. It takes the good fight of faith when enduring this process as well as patience and faith in Jesus to hold on to the victory Jesus has already won for us.

We are told to renew our minds and this is our responsibility. The reason why we are to renew our minds is because the words that we speak are formed first in our minds as pictures or audible words. That passes through our spirit, then we speak them out of our mouth. That is why children of God's Kingdom must renew their mind so that they begin to talk and say what pleases their King Jesus. Therefore, the devil will come up against you every chance he gets to throw you off after you make Jesus the Lord of your life. He does this by planting thoughts in your mind to try to get you to fall into his snares and traps in order to convince you that you are still a part of his family. You must stand against these attacks by confessing the truth of God's Word and standing in the midst of every circumstance by the power of His Spirit with confidence in Him; knowing that victory is already won through Jesus' death, resurrection and life.

The devil will come up against you every chance he gets to throw you off after you make Jesus the Lord of your life. He does this by planting thoughts in your mind to try to get you to fall into his snares and traps in order to convince you that you are still a part of his family.

Romans 8:6 says; ***For to be carnally minded is death; but to be spiritually minded is life and peace (Kjv).*** After meditating on this verse, I asked the Lord to give me insight on this verse. He said, ***the verse shows how the mind*** *of man dictates his life. If the man's mind is sound, then the man is able to bring about change, and he is able to show forth the praise of him that sent him. This is the one that hears and sees exactly what the Father is doing. This one knows that life and death are in the power of the tongue. It is only to them that wait who can find this place and to them that seek. Anyone who is willing to hear will hear.* Then I begin to read what He had spoke to me and I was attempting to understand what He had said to me with my own logic. Then I asked the Lord for more understanding and He said, *the verse is not to be understood with your mind it is to be understood with your heart. Your mind will become renewed, and it is your heart that will renew it. Both of them shall be one. It takes time for growth in these areas; they do not happen overnight.* Then I began to read what He had said and I had a question forming in my heart about what He said about *"my heart will renew my mind"* and before I could even ask the Lord, He answered me by saying, *the heart of the learned teacheth his mouth.* This verse is found in Proverbs 16:23 in the Bible and it says, *"The heart of the wise teacheth his mouth, and addeth learning to his lips (Kjv)."* I'd already known that out of the abundance of the heart the mouth speaks, so this helped me to know that this was Him speaking to me (Matthew 12:34). When the Lord speaks to us, our mind will always check and see if the words the Lord speaks in our heart line up with what His Word says. If our minds are not convinced that this is the Lord, we will not receive what He is saying to us, even if it is Him. Therefore, it is really important to renew our minds that we might hear and know that this is the Lord that is speaking to us. This spoken word in my heart had me amazed because the wisdom that He was giving me was helping me to understand this process of renewing my mind better. It would take time and I had to wait and to seek Him continuously to be in the place I desired in order to become spiritually minded. After He gave me insight on the verse and helped me understand it better he said, *Happy is he that findeth wisdom* and I laughed (Proverbs 3:13, Kjv). I love spending time with the Lord and when He teaches me His Word. He is so smart, loving and gentle. He makes this process of renewing your mind which is hard and very difficult at times, easy to deal with and fun.

This process can get frustrating when God allows Satan to attack His children's minds, and at times it seems like we are being defeated because of the things the enemy is constantly throwing at us as we stand for Christ. However, God is using this process to produce patience in our life, to purge us and to get us in a deeper and more intimate relationship with Jesus. The suffering that every child of the Kingdom has to endure is necessary in order to bring glory to our Father and to die to ourselves. *In Him we live, in Him we move, and in Him we have our being. If we suffer with Him, the Bible says that we shall also reign with Him (Acts 17: 28, 2 Timothy 2:12, Kjv)*. Knowing this, we are able to prevail and overcome in every area where the enemy comes against us.

The beauty of this process is that it produces patience in our lives.

God is using this process to produce patience in our life, to purge us and to get us in a deeper and more intimate relationship with Jesus.

Furthermore, when it is complete, we become established as sons in His Kingdom, perfect and complete, wanting nothing and only speaking what our Father has said.

James 1:2-4 says ***My brethren, count it all joy when ye fall into divers temptations; Knowing this, that the trying of your faith worketh patience. But let patience have her perfect work, that ye may be perfect and entire, wanting nothing (Kjv).***

The children of the World suffer without the benefit behind the children in God's kingdom. They suffer ignorantly because the good news about the Kingdom of God has been hid and their minds have been blinded to the truth by Satan. In 2 Corinthians 4:3 the Word of God says, ***But if our gospel be hid, it is hid to them that are lost: In whom the god of this world hath blinded the minds of them which believe not, lest the light of the glorious gospel of Christ, who is the image of God, should shine unto them (Kjv).***

The children of The World are convinced that they are living in freedom and liberty outside of God's Kingdom because their minds have been blinded. They have been tricked into believing that God's Kingdom is a religion with a bunch of do's and don'ts that make life boring and puts you in bondage. Because of this lie, they are stuck in bondage and are not able to experience the abundant life that Jesus came to give all men who would change their mind. This would change what they say and give them the opportunity to enter into God's Kingdom by being born again.

Proverbs 6:2 says; *You art snared by the words of your mouth; You are taken by the words of thy mouth (Nkjv).* Satan knows that in order to keep the children of the World trapped and in bondage, they must keep saying things that agree with his lies. In order to make them continue to make the wrong decisions and choices, they must keep on saying the opposite of what God has said. However, he also knows that if they change their mind by the grace of God, then eventually they are going to start saying what God has said. This is going to cause them to live in freedom, to make the right decisions and to make the right choices. The Word of God says in John 8:36 *Therefore If the Son make you free, you shall be free indeed (Kjv).*

Satan knows that in order to keep the children of the World trapped and in bondage, they must keep saying things that agree with his lies.

Furthermore, words are the essence of who we are. The Bible says in Proverbs 23:7 *For as he thinketh in his*

heart, so is he *(Kjv)*. The words a person speaks or the unspoken word that a person keeps in his heart makes him who he is. From the abundance of the heart the mouth speaks. You Are What You Speak. Jesus came and He only spoke what His Father told Him to speak. Jesus' Father filled Jesus' heart and His mind with His Word, and we know from the Scriptures that Jesus is one with God the Father. He was one with the Father on the Earth, He came from the Father and His heart and thoughts are the same as the Father's. That's how we become sons. For example, a farmer sows seeds into a field, then takes care of the seed by watering the field day and night so that the seed will one day grow and become good fruit that can one day be profitable to him. Jesus does the same thing in our life. He planted His Word (His seed) into our hearts (our gardens), and the Holy Spirit brings forth the harvest (good fruits) in our hearts (our gardens) by watering us as we read and meditate His Word day and night. This causes us to be filled with our Heavenly Father's thoughts, just like Jesus was on the Earth, and it makes us His son. This also causes us to speak what has been planted in our hearts in abundance, and that is what He speaks.

You are what you speak.

This same concept works with the World and that is why the enemy promotes things that get you to say the wrong things. Over and over again in your bedroom or in school, you are repeating things that are turning you into what you are saying. The words (the seeds) Satan uses are planted into your heart (your garden), and his evil spirits bring forth and harvest (bad fruits) in your heart (your garden). That causes you to be filled with Satan's thoughts which are lies, and that causes you to speak and say what he says and become a child of the World. Think for a moment of some of the things that you have repeated off of the television, off of your favorite CD or from your friends. The trap is that the more you repeat those words, the more you believe them and ultimately become the words you say.

The trap is that the more you repeat those words, the more you believe them and ultimately become the words you say.

We learned this truth from the Word of God, in Romans 10:17 that says, ***so then faith comes by hearing, and hearing by the word of God*** *(Nkjv)*. So as a child in the Kingdom of God, we know that the more we meditate on God's Word and by continuing to repeat it out loud to ourselves, our faith grows. The more we speak His words when we are with friends or family members, the more our faith grows. The more we keep God's Word in our mouth, the more we believe what He has said. Therefore, the same thing is true when people repeat over and over again the things they see on TV or listen to on the radio.

The more we keep God's Word in our mouth, the more we believe what He has said.

People subconsciously become adapted to or conformed to what they are repeating out of their mouths. This becomes their belief system, how their relationships go and eventually this becomes the norm for them and the truth becomes foolishness. They hold to the things in this world that lead to a bad outcome. They are ignorant of their outcome and take on the same attitude when confronted by the truth. They say, "I don't care, it's my life and I'll do what I want to with it; I'm grown, and nobody can tell me what to do."The words that they kept repeating day in and day out they now accept as their own words, their personality becomes framed by their words and their life now has become a reflection of their words.

In the Word of God in Hosea 4:6, God states, *My people are destroyed for lack of knowledge (kjv).* Not knowing that WORDS are also a WORLD that we choose to live in can cause us to make the wrong choice as well. In James 3:6, it mentions the tongue and it says, *the tongue is a fire, a WORLD of iniquity: so is the tongue among our members, that it defileth the whole body and setteth on fire the course of nature; and it is set on fire of hell (Kjv).*

This gives us a brief description on how powerful our tongues are. This verse says our tongue is a World of iniquity with the ability to destroy our life. This destruction occurs when the language that we use when we speak is of the World. In the Kingdom of God, there is a different language than in the World. The World can hear what we say, but it cannot understand what we are saying. The World can see the works and deeds that we do, but it cannot perceive what we are doing. Jesus said it this way in John 3:8, *The wind blows where it wishes, and you hear the sound of it, but cannot tell where it comes from and where it goes. So is every one born of the Spirit (Nkjv).*

Those that are born of the Spirit are children of the Kingdom of God. The words they speak are spirit and they are life, and they can only be spiritually discerned. On the earth, the children of the Kingdom speak a heavenly language that ushers the heavens on the earth so that their heavenly Father's will is done and His kingdom is established. Their speech is common to their Lord's speech. Jesus said in John 6:63: *the words that I speak unto you, they are spirit, and they are life (Kjv).* What Jesus is saying is that His words are alive and whoever hears them and do what they say to do WILL LIVE.

Jesus words are alive and whoever hears them and do what they say to do will live.

In James 3:4, the Word of God gives another look at the tongue and what it has the ability to do. It likens the tongue to a ship and its small rudder. *Look also at ships: although they are so large and are driven by fierce winds, they are turned by a very small rudder wherever the pilot desires (Nkjv).* James lets us know by this example that where ever our tongues go, that is where our bodies will eventually go. Our tongues can lead us to life or our tongues can lead us to death. We decide where we want to go by the words we choose to speak on a day- to-day basis. We must take responsibility for our words, the conversations we choose to have and the things we choose to say. Nobody makes us do or say anything; we choose.

The devil suggests things to our minds to see if we will hearken to his words. That is the only power he has. It lies in you believing and hearkening to his lies which are through the words he speaks. At times, he draws out a picture in order to trick or deceive you by planting a thought in your mind. But you have a choice. Many have chosen to believe they are homosexuals, that they are lesbians, that they are stupid, dumb or failures in life because of words that the devil has put in their mind that they believed. Once they believe what he lied to them about, then they begin to say what he said, and they become the words that he said. Until they choose to believe God's Words, say them and become who He says they are, they are trapped.

God's Word clearly states that we are not

homosexuals, lesbians, stupid, dumb or failures, but we are fearfully and wonderfully made in God's image and His likeness. We find out more about who we are by finding out more about who God is. The same is when you are looking at a product and trying to figure out what the product is capable of, what the product is and what the product is made up of. The best person to go and ask is the person who made the product.

We find out more about who we are by finding out more about who God is.

God knows us, He knows us very well and the Word of God says that even **the very hairs of your head are all numbered** in Matthew 10:30 (Kjv). He knows us better than anyone else; He made us, and therefore, whenever we are trying to figure out who we are, the best place to go is to Him.

He knows us better than anyone else; He made us, and therefore, whenever we are trying to figure out who we are, the best place to go is to Him.

The Word of God says in James 1:5-7: **If any of you lack wisdom, let him ask of God, that giveth to all men liberally, and upbraideth not; and it shall be given him. But let him ask in faith, nothing wavering. For he that wavereth** *is like a wave of the sea driven with the wind and tossed. For let not that man think that he shall receive any thing of the Lord (Kjv).*

God is willing to give us wisdom so that we will know who we are. This will help us know how to conduct ourselves and how we should speak. The wisdom that He is promising to give to us is freely given by Him, and after He gives it to us, He will not take it away from us. The only thing He is asking of us is that when we ask, we are confident that He will give it to us.

The Bible tells us in John 1:1-4: *In the beginning was the Word, and the Word was with God, and the Word was God. The same was in the beginning with God. All things were made by him; and without him was not anything made that was made. In him was life; and the life was the light of men (Kjv).* This Word that John is writing about was the living Word of God, Jesus Christ. He describes Jesus as the Word. Then he declares that the Word was God. He is letting his readers know, inspired by the Holy Spirit that Jesus, the anointed Word of God was with God in the beginning and with Jesus, God the Father made all things. He is expressing to us that Jesus, the Son of God, is the maker of Heaven and Earth, and all that is, and all that was and all that will ever be. He is the container that holds life, and all those who choose to drink out of His container will have life as well.

John goes on to say in verse five… *And the light shineth in darkness; and the darkness comprehended it not.*

The word shined in darkness means that it shined in places that did not understand, in places of ignorance, it exposed the lies and it unfolded the truth. It revealed the secrets that had been hid in the darkness and turned the darkness into light. This is the same way that God did in the beginning,

And the earth was without form, and void; and darkness was upon the face of the deep. And the Spirit of God moved upon the face of the waters. And God said, Let there be light: and there was light *(Genesis 1:2-3, Kjv).* The darkness did not understand, perceive, know, or comprehend the light. It is the same way that the World cannot comprehend the Kingdom of God. The Kingdom of God is a Kingdom of Words. God's Kingdom is a government upheld by His law that is the very Words He speaks. That is why the World has made a mockery of words and has twisted and perverted speech and language because Satan, the prince of the World, knows that the words that we speak become the world we know, and the world we know becomes the life we pursue.

God's Kingdom is a government upheld by His law that is the very Words He speaks.

We are subjected to the things that we do and the things we do are linked to the things we have allowed in our hearts. We act based upon a thought that comes from words in our heart or words put in our hearts. The words that we accept are the words that govern our lives and the words that we live by. Jesus said when tempted by the devil in the garden, *Man shall not live by bread alone, but by every word that proceedeth out of the mouth of God (Matthew 4:1, Kjv)*. The children in the Kingdom of God are those who are determined to live by and be ruled by only those words that come out of the mouth of their heavenly Father. They will renounce every other word that is not from Him.

The words that we accept are the words that govern our lives and the words that we live by.

The Kingdom of God or **The World**, *You are a part of one or the other, there is no in between.* You can be fooled to think that you do what you want and say what you want, but that is exactly how Satan operates in the World and tried to operate in Heaven. He did not want to let God continue to lead him; therefore, he decided that he would lead himself and that is when he fell. All individuals who do this are his followers, his children, his family and they fall too.

When Satan was in Heaven, he changed his words and that is when his life changed and his world changed. He could no longer be in the heavens because the heavens had only one King, God Himself. As soon as Satan's words changed to self-centeredness and pride, he was kicked out of Heaven because he no longer agreed with what God had said and was saying; therefore, he could no longer stay in Heaven. He chose a different way. He developed a broad system in the World that is made of many kingdoms. These lie in wait to deceive man into believing something that is simply not true.

The way of God is narrow. It is simple. It is not complicated at all, but it takes humility and a teachable spirit to allow the Holy Spirit to lead us into all truth. You must be born again!!! We enter into this new life of the Kingdom as a newborn baby who is learning to talk in order to learn those things that are necessary to become a child and then one day a mature adult. Your mentality and mindset should be the same as Paul who said in 1 Corinthians 4:4, *I know nothing by myself...* Paul was saying the only things that he knows are those things which God by His grace has allowed him to know.

You must be born again!!!

Understanding is rooted in God. The Word of God says in Proverbs 1:7 **The fear of the Lord is the beginning of knowledge: but fools despise wisdom and instruction (Kjv).** As you reverence God's Word, you begin to gain knowledge and receive direction. The Word of God says in Psalms 119:105 that **His word is a lamp unto my feet, and a light unto my path** (Kjv). His Word gives direction and it is our life. It sustains us, guides us, protects us and keeps us in all of our ways. You shall stand only by trusting in what He has said, and by doing so you are saying that He is your rock and foundation, the builder of your house (life).

The World must stand on words that have no substance, words that eventually come to an end. But God's Words are eternal; they don't have an end nor a beginning; they are everlasting. Jesus said in Matthew 5:18 *For verily I say unto you, Till heaven and earth pass, one jot or one title shall in no wise pass from the law, till all be fulfilled (Kjv).* In other words, no Word Jesus has said will ever go undone or cease or fall, until it accomplishes what He sent it to accomplish. His Word will always abide, every other word will perish.

Isaiah 55:11

So shall my word be that goeth forth out of my mouth: it shall not return unto me void, but it shall accomplish that which I please, and it shall prosper in the thing whereto I sent it *(Kjv).*

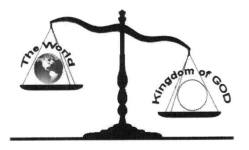

Chapter 5

The Natural and The Spiritual

1 Corinthians 2:14

But the natural man does not receive the things of the Spirit of God, for they are foolishness to him; nor can he know them, because they are spiritually discerned (Nkjv).

The things of God cannot be comprehended based on man's wisdom or man's knowledge; they are spiritually discerned. It doesn't matter if you read every Bible ever written, every book on knowing God or if you are smarter than Albert Einstein, you cannot know the things of God without His Spirit. The only way to understand the things of God is by the Spirit of God. In 1 Corithians 2:11-12 it says, *For what man knows the things of a man except the spirit of the man which is in him? Even so no one knows the things of God except the Spirit of God (Nkjv)*. The Holy Spirit is the only one who can bring man to a place of knowing what God is saying to His people. He uses spiritual Teachers, Pastors, Evangelists, Prophets, and Apostles that He has called to make His ways known to His people. These individuals are filled with His Holy Spirit and are lead by the Holy Spirit on how to make His ways easy to comprehend for others. This way all people would become spiritual and live a life of freedom in intimacy with the Father.

When we receive Jesus Christ as the Lord of our life, that is the beginning of our new life; at that moment our spirit came alive. Before, we were dead because of the trespasses of Adam in the garden, when he sinned against God; that is when we all died and became carnal because we were all in Adam. In Genesis 2:1,16-17 it says,

Thus the heavens and the earth were finished, and all the host of them. And the LORD God commanded the man, saying, Of every tree of the garden thou mayest freely eat: But of the tree of the knowledge of good and evil, thou shalt not eat of it: for in the day that thou eatest thereof thou shalt surely die (Kjv).

When Eve and Adam disobeyed God, they died. They were no longer alive yet they lived on after that without life. Their spirits were no longer alive, in fellowship or in agreement with God. From that day on, they lived according to the natural realm, not according to the spiritual realm. They fell out of fellowship with God who is life and the source of all living. When that happened, their life was subject to vanity, disaster and became meaningless.

They could only perceive and understand things based on their own knowledge and understanding. They were not able to go beyond what they saw because they now lived based on their own ability and strength. They began to trust in a lie and to live by a lie rather than trust in the truth and live by the truth. They believed what the enemy had made appear to be the truth when it was a lie. The knowledge that was given to them was the knowledge that they began to live by which brought forth death repeatedly in their lives.

The only way that this could stop was for the promise that God made to Eve to come to pass. This way, man would no longer just live on the earth following after vanity, but he would be back in relationship with God and have life filled with meaning and purpose. In Genesis 3:15 God said, *I will put enmity between you and the woman, And between your seed and her Seed: He shall bruise your head, and you shall bruise His heel (Nkjv).*

Jesus was this seed which would take man from his natural state of death back to his original state of life in God's image. Jesus was the seed that God the Father planted into the earth to die, break the power of sin off of humanity and to restore the relationship He had with man that Adam had lost with Him in the garden. He is the seed that birth a new creation of people that would stem from Him and live by him. In 2 Corinthians 5:17, it reads, *Therefore if any man be in Christ, he is a new creature: old things are passed away; behold, all things are become new (Kjv). That which is born of the flesh is flesh, and that which is born of the spirit is spirit (John 3:6, Nkjv).* Every child of God was born again from this spiritual seed that God the Father planted which is Jesus.

The natural man cannot understand or know the ways of God or the benefits and promises given to man because they are spiritually discerned. Therefore, he never can come to a place of understanding of what is so easy to see for individuals who are spiritual (born again), and that is that there is no comparison between the Kingdom of God and the World. The spiritual individual is able to judge correctly and see this plainly because he is filled with God's Spirit and governed by Him. In 1 Corinthians 2:15 it says, *he that is spiritual judgeth all things, yet he himself is judged of no man (Kjv).* Because of the spiritual man's connection with the Holy Spirit he is able to give a correct judgment in every area of natural and spiritual people's lives. He judges according to what the Lord reveals to him about different areas in people's lives. Jesus put it this way in John 5:30: *I can of mine own self do nothing: as I hear, I judge: and my judgment is just; because I seek not mine own will, but the will of the Father which hath sent me (Kjv).* Spiritual people in the Kingdom of God judge the same way that Jesus judged when he lived on the earth. When they hear from the Holy Spirit speaking in their heart, they judge.

In Romans 8:16 it says, *The Spirit itself beareth witness with our spirit, that we are children of God.* Therefore, we can know and judge the things of God properly because He makes them known to us. We have the privilege in the Kingdom of God to fellowship with Him and embrace His wisdom and knowledge as He teaches us. This happens when we receive Jesus as our Lord and ask our heavenly Father for His Holy Spirit that His Son Jesus promised would come and would guide us into all truth. In John 16:13 it says, *when he, the Spirit of truth, is come, he will guide you into all truth: for he shall not speak of himself; but whatsoever he shall hear, that shall he speak: and he will shew you things to come (Kjv).*

Jesus sent us the Holy Spirit to make His ways known to us so that we will not live any longer in darkness, but in His light; the light that lights every man that enters the world and the light that shines in every place (John 1:9), revealing truth to everyone He encounters in hope of an embrace from each person He finds. He looks desperately for anyone who would believe so that He can change them into the person that He created them to be.

The one who reveals these things is the Holy Spirit, the Spirit of Life. He gives each of us the opportunity to be light in a world full of darkness and despair. This is so that we might show the world the person, the man, Christ Jesus, that died as we give our lives daily so that He can live and be manifested in us. We have hope that He alone will be glorified by our life and that we would please Him in all that we do as we are transformed from the natural and carnal state to the spiritual and holy state.

Romans 8:6-8 says: **to be carnally minded is death; but to be spiritually minded is life and peace. Because the carnal mind is enmity against God: for it is not subject to the law of God, neither indeed can be. So then they that are in the flesh cannot please God (Kjv).**

We have two different types of outlooks on life. One is the outlook from the carnal man, and the other is the outlook from the spiritual man. These outlooks are completely opposite. One looks at the things he sees to determine the way things are, and the other looks at the things that are not seen and knows the way things really are. The one trust and believes in God's Word and the other trusts and believes the words of others, his own words and the devil's over the Word of God. For example, Eve listen to the voice of Satan, Adam listen to the voice of Eve and both of them died because of it.

What the Scriptures mean by death is a state of a person that is separated from God, not in communion with Him and not in right relationship with Him. We are all incomplete without Him, and there will always be a void in our hearts when we do not have Him. Therefore, those who are carnally minded will always experience death on their journey in life because their journey does not include Him.

However, those who have received Jesus have received also His Spirit and have entered into a right relationship, communion and fellowship with Him, and they always experience life and peace because He is with them and they are with Him on their journey in life.

We are all incomplete without Him, and there will always be a void in our hearts when we do not have Him.

In Romans 8:6, the people that are carnally minded are people against God and are governed by the World and its system. They cannot follow God's law which is His Word nor do they come under His government which is His Kingdom. They have decided not to do things His way, but their own way. Proverbs 14:12 says, *there is a way which seemeth right unto a man, but the end thereof are the ways of death (Kjv).* Not following God's pathway no matter how it looks or appear in life will always be the wrong path and lead to death.

One day while I was studying, the Holy Spirit spoke to me and said, *"If you live according to your carnal nature, you shall die, but if you live according to the Spirit of God, you shall live."*

I looked the word "according" up in Oxford American Writer's Thesaurus and I found that it means: as stated by or in, in a manner corresponding or conforming, and in proportion or relation to. The Holy Spirit was revealing to me that if you live in agreement, in harmony, under the rules and standard of the carnal nature, you will die. One reason is that the carnal natured man does not seek guidance nor heed the instruction from God. However, if you live in agreement, in harmony, under the rules and standards of the Spirit of God, you will live. Your life would be filled with meaning, purpose, joy, peace, love, patience, hope and faith which are all found in Him.

If you live in agreement, in harmony, under the rules and standards of the Spirit of God, you will live.

We have been taught growing up in the World that the ways of God are boring and too hard to follow. However, Jesus said in Matthew 11:30: ***my yoke is easy, and my burden is light*** *(Kjv)*. We know that He is not going to put on us more than we can bear and even while we are carrying the burden that He gives us, He is there with us all the way to help us carry it (1 Cor. 10:13).

The reality is that to follow God's ways, to come into fellowship with Him, to become spiritual by receiving His Spirit and taking time to meditate to renew your mind is the most awesome and fulfilling life that anyone can live. In His presence is the fullness of joy, and He is the most loving and adorable Father anyone could ever come to know. The truth is that ***we love Him, because He first loved us*** (1Jh 4:19, Kjv).

Those that truly love Jesus are spiritual individuals who have seen His love for them and experienced His love for them. Because of this, they fell in love with Him, and there is nothing that they will not do for Him because of His love for them.

Nevertheless, you must be born again. Jesus said to Nicodemus in John 3:3 *except a man be born again, he cannot see the kingdom of God (Kjv)*. To be born again is to enter into the new life Jesus promised by faith in Him alone. Jesus said that *I am come that they might have life, and that they might have it more abundantly* in John 10:10 (Kjv). The life that Jesus came to give us is a life of victory where all our sins have been forgiven and taken away from us. Now we live in Him and are no longer sinners, but now we are righteous. We are free from guilt, free from shame and sin shall not have dominion over us because we are not under the law, but under grace (Roman 6:14). As children in the Kingdom, we now have the privilege of reckoning ourselves dead to sin and alive to Christ. We now see ourselves in Him and Him in us. This is a new place that we have been positioned in where we are given a life that allows us to experience Heaven while living on Earth.

In 2 Corinthians 5:17 the Word of God says, *If any man be in Christ, he is a new creature: old things are passed away; behold, all things are become new (Kjv).*

The children in the Kingdom are new creations in Christ Jesus and are *being born again, not of corruptible seed but of incorruptible, by the word of God that liveth and abideth for ever* according to 1 Peter 1:23 (Kjv). The children in the Kingdom of God have passed from death to life by the finished work of Jesus Christ on the cross. Jesus has already won the battle for us, now we celebrate in His victory by proclaiming what He has already done for us as we fight the good fight of faith. The good fight of faith is a fight of knowledge that we must hold to each and every day; the knowledge is the very words Jesus speaks.

2 Corinthians 10:4 lets us know, *the weapons of our warfare are not carnal, but mighty through God to the pulling down of strong holds; to the casting down imagination, and every high thing that exalt itself against the knowledge of God, and bringing into captivity every thought to the obedience of Christ (Kjv).*

What we must all recognize is that it is all about knowledge-who are you going to believe, the devil and the World or God and His Kingdom. You are going to have to make a choice to stay carnal and live in sin by giving in to the lust in the World or to be born again and become spiritual and live free from sin. Romans 8:2 lets us know, *for the law of the Spirit of life in Christ Jesus hath made me free from the law of sin and death.* We are free from sin and death once we decide to be born again and to enter into the Kingdom of God.

What we must all recognize is that it is all about knowledge-who are you going to believe, the devil and the World or God and His Kingdom.

Jesus said in John 3:5-6 ***Verily, verily, I say unto thee, Except a man be born of water and of the Spirit, he cannot enter into the kingdom of God. That which is born of the flesh is flesh; and that which is born of the Spirit is spirit.***

To enter the Kingdom, you must be born of water and of the Spirit. The water symbolizes the Word of God and the Spirit symbolizes His Holy Spirit which we all receive when we receive Him. The water and God's Spirit work together and help us to enter into the Kingdom of God by truth and grace. There is absolutely no other way to enter into this new life without God's Word and His Spirit. God's Word is the law in His Kingdom that we must uphold and be governed by and His Spirit is our comforter, helper, protector and our guide who leads us into all truth by revealing to us what God is really saying in His Word.

Now, that which is born of the flesh is the carnal man who refuses or rejects the knowledge of our King, Jesus, to enter into the Kingdom of God. As I mentioned earlier, those who are born of the Spirit are those who have received Jesus as their Savior and have received His Holy Spirit, and they are no longer carnal, but now they are spiritual. They choose to be governed by the Word of God, to renew their minds by meditating on God's Word and to be careful to follow and do everything that is written in it as they are led by His Spirit.

The children of the Kingdom know that to be born again is to live a life separated from sin, from defeat, from guilt and from lack. It is a life of Heaven on Earth. However, the only way to experience this life is to become born again and enter into a one on one personal relationship with Jesus Christ. FOR TO KNOW HIM IS ETERNAL LIFE. John 17:3 says, ***And this is life eternal, that they might know thee the only true God, and Jesus Christ, whom thou hast sent (Kjv).***

The only way to experience this life is to become born again and enter into a one on one personal relationship with Jesus

---

John 4:24

God is a Spirit: and they that worship him must worship him in spirit and in truth *(Kjv).*

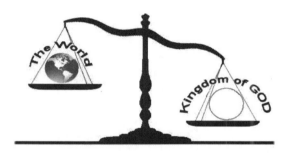

Chapter 6

Mistaken Identity

Romans 1:16, 17

For I am not ashamed of the gospel of Christ, for it is the power of God to salvation for everyone who believes, for the Jew first and also for the Greek. For in it the righteousness of God is revealed from faith to faith; as it is written, "The just shall live by faith" (Kjv).

As I began to read this passage written by the Apostle Paul, the Holy Spirit began to reveal to me exactly what it was refering to. He spoke to me and said, *It is relating to the past, how God made man and how man through his connection with God was able to live. This account that Paul was writing about showed how man's connection with God caused man to live in a place of reverence because his faith was found in God. The only reason man was able to live in this place of reverence was because his faith was in God; he had the God kind of faith.*

For so many years, we have been taught that we are everything but who we really are. We have believed many things that have been said about us, and we have believed many things as a result of our own experiences and failures. However, the only way to see the true you is through a relationship in connection with God. <u>In Him is where your true identity is, along with your faith to believe that this is the real you.</u> Your connection with Him is far more glorious than anything else you can think of connecting with. It is the best life you can ever live, and nothing else comes close.

The only way to see the true you is through a relationship in connection with God.

Without a relationship with God, you will look at the World and say that this is the best for me because you will never be able to come to grips with who you are. You will always be satisfied with less than you are supposed to have if you never figure out who you are. You will never reach your potential or never fulfill your purpose in life until you figure out who you are. The World will continue to move forward and you will always be standing in place because before you can understand what you should be doing or where you should be, you must know your own identity.

You will never reach your potential or never fulfill your purpose in life until you figure out who you are.

The truth has not been hidden from any of us. We all have an opportunity to come to a place of recognizing who we are. However, many people in the world today have decided that the person they see when they look in the mirror is not the person they want to be. We must all come from under the covers and be willing to accept ourselves as we are; for we are fearfully and wonderfully made. We are the apple of God's eye; we are magnificently crafted and formed by brilliantly delicate hands. We are the best God has to offer in the world, and we should be proud that we are who we are and not try to discover anything other than our true identity.

We are the best God has to offer in the world, and we should be proud that we are who we are and not try to discover anything other than our true identity.

The World will make you feel like you have to do something else and that who you are isn't good enough. You must establish or make an identity for yourself so that you will be noticed or recognized. You need to show others that you are different, that you are not like everybody else. This will have you putting tattoos all over your body, piercings, acting out a fake personality or pretending to be someone who you are not.

The truth is that there is nobody like you in the entire world. You are unique, you are special, you are important and you are somebody. Nobody is exactly like you; God made you the way you are to please Him. The World wants you to please everybody but God, and it tries to encourage you to change from being you. The more you are you, the more you will be satisfied with your life. The more you try to be somebody else, the less satisfied you will be.

You are unique, you are special, you are important and you are somebody. Nobody is exactly like you; God made you the way you are to please Him.

The World wants people to think that their value is in what they have, in how they look, in who they know, in where they have been, and in what they have achieved. When the reality is that your value is in who made you. Think about it, God's value of you was so much that He sent Jesus Christ, His Son, to die for your sins so that you and Him can be back in relationship together. God sees you as so valuable that He sent Jesus to die in your place. This should help you begin to see how valuable you really are, and make you want to know more about yourself.

Your value is in who made you.

Where you grew up does not say anything about who you are. Who your parents are, where you went to school, where you graduated from, how much money you have, and where you work says little about who you are. These things are what you have experienced that has nothing to do with who you are as a person. You are who you were created to be. Not what you chose to be or decided to be. Our identity is rooted in our maker. Only He knows what He made. Others can look and see something else when they look at you, you can see yourself as someone else, but God knows exactly what He made when He formed you. That is why it is important to look past what appears to be true and grasp what is really true. The truth is that no matter what you have done or are doing can change what God has said about you and who you are in His eyes.

You are who you were created to be. Not what you chose to be or decided to be. Our identity is rooted in our maker. Only He knows what He made.

In John 8:32, Jesus declared that ***If you continue in my word, then are you my disciples indeed; And you shall know the truth, and the truth shall make you free (Kjv).***

Wisdom cries in the street, waiting for those who will hear her and come running. Jesus is waiting. Whoever will answer the knock at the door will find truth. Jesus said in Revelation 3:20, *Behold, I stand at the door, and knock: if any man hear my voice, and open the door, I will come in to him, and will sup with him, and he with me (Kjv).*

The opportunity to receive truth will always be open as long as we are alive; however, we will have forfeited our opportunity on the day that we die. Many believe that since they're still young, they should have fun now and do what they want, then turn to God when they get older. However, tomorrow is not promised to any man. Our opportunity for life is today. This is not something that we should put off because we must live realizing that today is the day that I must choose, and tomorrow I might not get the opportunity.

The children of the Kingdom of God made a choice. It was the best choice anyone in the world could make, and that choice was to be born again. The Bible says in John 3:6, *that which is born of the flesh is flesh; and that which is born of the Spirit is Spirit (Kjv).* The children of the Kingdom became born of the Spirit when they received Jesus as their Lord and when they asked their heavenly Father for the gift of His Holy Spirit that He promised to give to anyone who would repent and ask Him. That is when they became a new person. In 2 Corinthians 5:17, the Word of God says that: *if any man be in Christ, he is a new creature: old things are passed away; behold, all things are become new (Kjv).* From that moment on, everything in their life changed and they were no longer that person they use to be, but now they are sons of God, born of His Spirit.

In Luke 18:17 Jesus proclaims, *Assuredly, I say to you, whoever does not receive the Kingdom of God as a little child will by no means enter it (Nkjv)*. In order to agree with God in everything that He has said and says, you have to reject and renounce everything that you believed before and become a child that you might become wise and enter into His Kingdom. Our heavenly Father is the most brilliant, wise and all-knowing Person in the Universe. Therefore, we become wise when we forget what we learned before and become as a child and open up ourselves to learn from Him, believe in Him and agree with Him. Then our identity is revealed through Him, not through what we have done or are doing but through who we belong to and come from.

Therefore, we become wise when we forget what we learned before and become as a child and open up ourselves to learn from Him, believe in Him and agree with Him.

Once each of us has made a choice to be born again, we no longer have a mistaken identity. We know and learn to know who we are through Him, and His truth makes us free from every lie as His Holy Spirit leads us and guides us into all truth. This alone will cause us to see the Kingdom of God and the World as it really is, under the government of God's

Kingdom which is ruled by God's children.

Everything in our life becomes new as we continue in the Word of God which proves that we are students of our great Teacher, Jesus Christ. We are constantly walking in the newness of life as we yield to the nature of God and the desires of God's Holy Spirit. This is a complete change in thinking and in deeds, just as a baby goes from crawling, to walking, to running, it takes time. However, it happens, and the one who is doing it in and through us is God.

This is a complete change in thinking and in deeds, just as a baby goes from crawling, to walking, to running, it takes time.

Philippians 2:12-13

Wherefore, my beloved, as ye have always obeyed, not as in my presence only, but now much more in my absence, work out your own salvation with fear and trembling. For it is God which worketh in you both to will and to do of his good pleasure (Kjv).

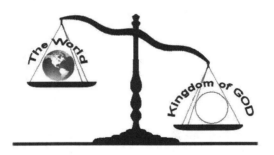

Chapter 7

Dominion Over The Earth

Psalms 8:4-6

What is man that You are mindful of him, And the son of man that You visit him? For You have made him a little lower than the angels, And You have crowned him with glory and honor. You have made him to have dominion over the works of Your hands; You have put all things under his feet (Nkjv).

We were born to rule. We were not born to allow evil things to take place in our life or in this world and to do nothing about it. The children in the Kingdom of God understand this: that God gave us power to control and enforce what happens in our life and in the World. In the beginning, God gave man dominion over the earth:

And God said, Let us make man in our image, after our likeness: and let them have dominion over the fish of the sea, and over the fowl of the air, and over the cattle, and over all the earth, and over every creeping thing that creepeth upon the earth (Gen. 1:26, Kjv).

Now when God gave us this dominion over the earth and everything in it, it clearly reveals our relationship with Him. It shows how He trusted us to take good care of it, and how He expects an expansion and multiplication of what He has given to us. Before our heavenly Father gave us anything, He gave us an understanding that when someone is given something, it is no longer the other person's responsibility. The earth belongs to us because He has given it to us; however, it is still His because it is a part of His kingdom, but we are responsible for it. We must make sure that everything on it and in it is the way He likes it. What we allow on the earth and whatever we don't allow on the earth, God is holding us responsible for.

We must make sure that everything on it and in it is the way He likes it. What we allow on the earth and whatever we don't allow on the earth, God is holding us responsible for.

The children in the Kingdom take joy in looking after this territory (the earth) that their King has given them, and they make decrees daily concerning it, based on what they will allow and will not allow. They have been entrusted with great authority and power from God to fulfill His purpose on the earth. His purpose is to bring the whole earth under the government of Heaven.

The children of the Kingdom rule on the earth under the government of Heaven led by God's Holy Spirit. They rule by submitting to the Word of God and trusting in the Holy Spirit to use them to bring forth the Lord's glory on the earth. They are challenged in many ways, although they understand that the finished work of Jesus has already given them victory and complete dominion on the earth. They still have to stand their ground and fight the good fight of faith that they have been called to fight on behalf of the Kingdom of God. They enforce their rights and authority by swinging the sword of the Spirit, which is the Word of God against all opposition and enemies that attempt to set up any other kingdom in their territory.

The children of the Kingdom of God have the power within them to stop any and everything that is happening on the earth that is not like Heaven. Jesus, during his time on Earth, turned darkness into light everywhere He went and established His Father's kingdom, and they can too. He turned the World upside down by demonstrating His authority and dominion over the earth through the many signs and wonders He did. He even went beyond the laws of nature by walking on water and commanding the storm to be still because the laws in Heaven (the Kingdom of God) override the laws on the earth.

Jesus, during his time on Earth, turned darkness into light everywhere He went and established his Father's kingdom, and they can too.

The children in the Kingdom have the power to stop abortion, stop murders, stop theft, stop drug dealers, stop crimes, stop poverty, stop abuse, stop perversion, stop homosexuality and to stop fornication. The whole Earth belongs to them, and God has given them dominion and control; therefore, they don't have to allow these things to happen. The children of the World, however, are subject to them and do not have this dominion, because they refuse to acknowledge the Son of God, Jesus Christ, who gave the children in the Kingdom of God their dominion.

Some might question how it is that the children of the Kingdom of God are going to stop murders, drug dealers, abortions and so on.... They do it by ruling in the natural realm from the spiritual realm in prayer as they go before God and thank Him for the earth He has given them. Then they declare what shall be on the earth and what will not be allowed on the earth in specific details. When they speak in faith, it begins to happen immediately. While many might not believe this truth, sooner than they think, the whole earth and the heavens will be made new and all of ungodliness will perish (1 John 1:15-17). The main reason is because it is written in the Word of God and the children in the Kingdom prayed and made decrees that Heaven be on Earth.

The children in the Kingdom of God rule on the earth exactly like their Father in Heaven by calling those things that be not as though they were (Romans 4:17). They do this by saying what they desire and declaring what their heavenly Father has already said in His Word. This is how God uses some of them in prayer as they proclaim:

Father, I thank you for the dominion you have given me over all the earth. I take full responsibility for what you have given me and now I declare that there will be no more abortion in America. I declare that the drug dealers and users will turn from their drugs to You. I declare that the stronghold of homosexuality that has come over the young people in America is broken now in Jesus' Name. I declare peace, joy and righteousness now throughout America in the name of Jesus. Amen.

The children of the Kingdom of God have the power within them to change the World, and the more they take dominion on the earth, the more they walk in the destiny that God has called them to. The children of the World do not understand these things; they are blind to the truth of their own destiny and purpose on the earth because they have chosen not to see (2 Cor. 4:4).

In Luke 10:19, Jesus declared, *Behold, I give you the authority to trample on serpents and scorpions, and over all the power of the enemy, and nothing shall by any means hurt you (Nkjv)*. Once the children of the World decide to let Jesus open their eyes, then they will see that the men that are standing on the corner are not behind the drug operation, and the person buying the drugs is not the person behind the addiction. Although these people choose to do it, they were influenced by lying spirits that tricked them into believing their lies. When drug dealers and those addicted to drugs believe the thoughts that these lying spirits plant in their minds, they get caught in a stronghold. Thank God, we the children of the Kingdom are able to pull down strongholds and to remove the bondage that the enemy has put them in by declaring and decreeing their victory.

When drug dealers and those addicted to drugs believe the thoughts that these lying spirits plant in their minds, they get caught in a stronghold.

The world as we know it is not run by the things that we see or the people we see that seem to be in charge; there are spirits in the unseen realm in high places that are really in charge in the spiritual world. Many people are ignorant of these spirits, but the children of the Kingdom of God are not. They know that these spirits are real and that we are not fighting a war against people to reign and rule on the earth, but up against wicked and evil spirits. Ephesians 6:12 says, *For we wrestle not against flesh and blood, but against principalities, against powers, against the rulers of the darkness of this world against spiritual wickedness in high places. Wherefore take unto you the whole amour of God, that ye may be able to withstand in the evil day, and having done all, to stand (Kjv).*

The whole world lies in sin and wickedness because of those who are ruling over them. There was a very interesting encounter in the wilderness when the enemy came up to Jesus after He had fasted forty days and forty nights. The last thing that the enemy said to Jesus to try to bring Him under his authority on the earth in Matthew 4:8-9 reads: ***Again, the devil took Him up on an exceedingly high mountain, and showed Him all the kingdoms of the world and their glory. And he said to Him, All these things I will give you if You will fall down and worship me (Nkjv).***

The devil tried to convince Jesus, based on his influence over men on the earth, to worship him, but Jesus had His own influence that He was bringing on the earth (the Kingdom of God) to overthrow the devil's influence. However, look at the devil's statement, "*all these things I will give you.*" He is saying that every kingdom on the earth is influenced by him, that he is in control and if Jesus worshipped him, he would give Jesus control or influence over them. However, Jesus never fell for the plan that the enemy plotted against Him, and He defeated Satan when He died on the cross and took back complete control over the earth by paying for the sin of the World that caused Adam to lose the earth. This put man right back in his rightful place on the earth and now man is no longer subject to the works of the devil. 1 John 3:8 states, ***For this purpose The Son of God was*** *manifested, that he might destroy the works of the devil (Kjv).* Therefore, it is finished; we are freed by the power of Jesus Spirit and the washing of His blood.

The problem is that though everyone has been freed, only those who are in the Kingdom can perceive the truth, because the truth is only revealed to those who God reveals it to. He allows those who love the darkness to stay blind until they want to come to the light, and then they can see. Everything that is outside of the Kingdom of God is a part of Satan's influence and a part of Satan's kingdom. There are no in-betweens or no neutrals: You may think that you are not influenced by either, but you are. We must not think any other way but come to understand that if I am not for God, I am against Him, or if I am for God, then I am against Satan. We have to make a decision; we always have a choice to make in life, if we want to eat from the tree of life or the tree of the knowledge of good and evil. In other words, do we want to live life the way God intended in a real relationship with Him, or do we want to live any kind of way we want to, a part from God?

Everything that is outside of the Kingdom of God is a part of Satan's influence and a part of Satan's kingdom. There are no in-betweens or no neutrals: You may think that you are not influenced by either, but you are.

The natural realm displays only a glimpse of what is

taking place in the spirit realm, where the natural realm is dominated. We, who are born again, understand these things because we have the Spirit of God on the inside of us, and He teaches us how to rule and reign on the earth, which has been placed back into our hands to rule along side of Jesus our Lord. Those who are in the World under the dominion of sin and death will never rule but only be ruled by Satan, but we are heirs of God and joint heirs with Jesus Christ and we have an inheritance on the earth because we are sons of the King (Romans 8:17).

The things you see on the earth now are only temporary. It may look like the World is getting worse and worse in the natural realm which would suggest that the kingdom of Satan is defeating the Kingdom of God, however, no matter how it looks, the war is over; it is finished; Jesus already has defeated Satan and his kingdom. When He died and rose from the dead for the sins of the world, He took all authority and power from Satan and now reigns throughout all eternity in Heaven and on Earth. Through Him we are victorious permanently now and forevermore.

The war is over; it is finished; Jesus already has defeated Satan and his kingdom.

Furthermore, the World getting worse and worse was predicted by God in His Word, which clearly reveals to us who is in charge in 2 Timothy 3:1-5:

This know also, that in the last days perilous times shall come. For men shall be lovers of their own selves, covetous, boasters, proud, blasphemers, disobedient to parents, unthankful, unholy, Without natural affection, trucebreakers, false accusers, incontinent, fierce, despisers of those that are good, Traitors, heady, highminded, lovers of pleasures more than lovers of God; Having a form of godliness, but denying the power thereof: from such turn away (Kjv).

The children in the Kingdom have been given insight into these things and have been told to turn away. They know that it doesn't matter what things look like or how they appear, but that the Kingdom of God is going to continue to rule and reign on the earth through them. And what is this kingdom that we so gratefully take part in? In Romans 14:17 it says, *For the kingdom of God is not meat and drink; but righteousness, and peace, and joy in the Holy Ghost (Kjv).*

Mathew 28:18-20

And Jesus came and spake unto them, saying, All power is given to me in heaven and in earth. Go ye therefore, and teach all nations, baptizing them in the name of the Father, and of the Son, and of the Holy Ghost: Teaching them to observe all things whatsoever I have commanded you: and, lo, I am with you alway, even unto the end of the world. Amen (Kjv).

Chapter 8

The Storm

Mathew 7:24-27

Therefore whoever hears these sayings of Mine, and does them, I will liken him to a wise man who built his house on the rock: and the rain descended, and the floods came, and the winds blew and beat on that house; and it did not fall, for it was founded on the rock. But everyone who hears these sayings of Mine, and does not do them, will be like a foolish man who built his house on the sand: and the rain descended, the floods came, and the winds blew and beat on that house; and it fell. And great was its fall (Nkjv).

In these scriptures, Jesus points out that the storm is going to come and those that will listen to Him and do what

He says will survive the storm, all others will not. The children of the Kingdom of God and the children of the World are both going to have to face a storm one day or another. The storm might be the sudden death of a loved one, a drive by shooting, your mother and father giving you away, you getting really sick or you are raped or sexually abused. We all have to face something that we did not expect to face, and it is going to challenge who and what we put our trust in.

The Lord said that in the world, we (the children in the Kingdom of God) will have tribulation. This is a fact because we are the Lord's servants, and we follow His examples on the Earth. We are His instruments to bring forth His Kingdom by bearing fruit on the Earth that should remain forever. Our steps are ordered by Him and He shall receive all glory and honor as we grow and mature in His Kingdom into His complete image and likeness. In the Kingdom of God, the storm is our process to get us to the next place in Him; it also helps us to produce patience. In James 1:2-4 it says:

My brethren, count it all joy when you fall into various trials, knowing that the testing of your faith produces patience. But let patience have its perfect work, that you may be perfect and complete, lacking nothing (Nkjv).

In the Kingdom of God, we look at the things that we face and no matter how difficult they are, we end up counting it all joy because we know that all things are working together for our good because we love God and are called according to

His purpose (Romans 8:28). We have chosen to lay down our life on behalf of our King Jesus Christ in order to put on His life. We know that we will have to suffer, and we prepare to do so knowing that the suffering of this present time can't compare to the glory that shall be revealed in us (Romans 8:18).

We trust in His Word and His Word warns us that it is normal for things to happen that we might not understand. Whatever happens to us doesn't matter since our lives are not our own, we belong to Him. Therefore, in everything, we can rejoice, knowing that we already have victory because we put all of our trust in Him and rely completely on Him to help us through it all. Learning daily to put our trust in Him causes us to grow in faith and never look to anything or anyone to save us, except Jesus Christ alone.

Learning daily to put our trust in Him causes us to grow in faith and never look to anything or anyone to save us, except Jesus Christ alone.

The storm for the World reveals to them their false security and what they have believed in from the beginning. It is a horrible thing to be in an ongoing storm when you are a part of the World and not the Kingdom of God because there is no way out. Jesus began to preach in John 14:6 and He said, *I am the way, the truth, and the life: and no man cometh unto the father except by me (Kjv).* Jesus is the only way out of the storm that we all must deal with, and without Jesus, none of us would be able to stand against it.

There are some things many people would not tell anyone about because they allow their storm to stay a part of their life. This is because they have not found a cure to make it go away. We have all done something in our life that we are not proud of, some worse than others, and we all, just like Adam and Eve when they took the fig leaves, try to cover it up with the closest thing we can find. However, none of these things work. We are still naked and need someone to cloth us. The storm continues to beat against us until we finally surrender from trying to fight it alone and call on Jesus who has already defeated it for us.

The storm continues to beat against us until we finally surrender from trying to fight it alone and call on Jesus who has already defeated it for us.

In Mark 4:37-39 it says, ***And a great windstorm arose, and the waves beat into the boat, so that it was already filling. But He was in the stern, asleep on a pillow. And they awoke Him and said to Him, "Teacher, do You not care that we are perishing?" Then He arose and rebuked the wind, and said to the sea, "Peace, be still!" And the wind ceased and there was a great calm*** *(Nkjv)*.

The one who controls the storm is Jesus. He allowed the storm to come even at a time when He needed some rest. It didn't matter the time or the season, the storm came. He knew He had authority over it and the same goes for every child in His Kingdom. We understand that there may be something that happens that we don't expect, but we know that we have authority over every storm that comes. We only believe and trust in the midst of the storm that comes our way, knowing that victory is already ours.

We all have to realize that everything that happens in life happens for a reason. We can live a life outside of God's Kingdom, and by His goodness and mercy, He always seeks to draw men near. Therefore, He is constantly seeking for individuals who will see the storm for what it is, and it is a key for the ungodly as well as the Godly to grow in a closer relationship to Him. The key is that the storm must not be rejected; it must be accepted for the sinner and the World to realize that without God, there is absolutely no hope. For those who are in the Kingdom of God, our suffering brings forth glory. For as many as suffer with Him (that is Jesus), they shall be also gloried with Him (Romans 8:17).

The children of Israel had a problem in the Old Testament. They wanted the promise of God, but they didn't want to face the storm. The problem was that it was their Father who took them to the storm in order to get them to do what He called them to do when He gave them the promise. However, they didn't want to do things in His order or to submit to His process; they wanted to receive the promise without fighting for it. The truth is that the Israelite's would not have kept the promise because they were not willing to fight for it. If you are not willing to fight for the promise that God has given you, the promise is not worth enough in your eyes for you to posses. Until you are willing to face the storm, you are not willing to keep the promise. You might be willing to receive it, but it takes a fight to get it so that you will maintain it, treasure it and keep it.

If you are not willing to fight for the promise, the promise is not worth enough in your eyes. Until you are willing to face the storm, you are not willing to keep the promise.

In Hebrews 12:5 it says, **My son, do not despise the chastening of the Lord, Nor be discouraged when you are rebuked by Him; For whom the Lord loves He chastens, And scourges every son whom He receives. If you endure chastening, God deals with you as with sons; for what son is there whom a father does not chasten** (Nkjv)?

We all must recognize that most of the time when storms arise, we are being pushed to the other side of the sea, across the Jordan into the Promised Land. We are not being over burdened or over tried; we are being called to a higher place. The Word of the God says that He will not put more on you than you can bear. Therefore, the children in the Kingdom of God are always bearing burdens on the Earth until God's kingdom is established however, His burdens are light and his yoke is easy (Mathew 11:30). The World does not have such great and precious promises as we do because it is under another government and another system that is designed to over burden them and to bring them into complete destruction and eternal damnation.

In the Kingdom of God, our heavenly Father allows certain rough seasons in our life to purge us so that we will accomplish more than we have ever accomplished before. We learn to suffer even as Jesus learned to suffer and was obedient even unto death. That we too, will please our heavenly Father just like Jesus did by saying, "not my will, but your will be done Lord (Mathew 26:42)."

In every circumstance in our life, we have decisions and choices to make and the Word of God says in 1 Peter 3:17:*For it is better, if the will of God be so, that ye suffer for well doing, than for evil doing (Kjv).* Meaning, that it is far better to suffer when you have done something good than to suffer for doing something wrong. It is obvious, that individuals who choose to suffer for doing something right are living a life filled with purpose and meaning. These individuals have made it up in their mind that no matter what happens in their life, they are determined to continue to trust in the Lord. This faith that the children of the Kingdom of God have in God causes them to overcome all obstacles and boundaries in their life no matter how difficult or trying their storms appear.

The storm for those who are children of the Kingdom is not unusual for them, it is a normal lifestyle. However, they don't live by what they experience or by what takes place around them. They only live by faith based on what the King has decreed in His Word to be true. The storm has no control over them or doesn't move them. They are founded on a rock that cannot be moved by any man, that rock is Jesus Christ, the Son of God.

They are founded on a rock that cannot be moved by any man, that rock is Jesus Christ, the Son of God.

The position that the children of the Kingdom take is a position that has been given to them by their Father. The storm is not working against them, but working for them. The great thing about this is that they see the storm as it really is, because they know that God is in control and they can see the Kingdom of God. The Word of God in John 3:3 says, **Except a man be born again, he cannot see the kingdom of God** *(Kjv)*. The children in the Kingdom of God have been born again and they see through their new spiritual eyes, their eyes of faith exactly what the outcome of every storm in their life is going to be. They are confident that before the storm comes, they have already made it through it. Also, that the storm is design to bring glory to their Father and help them to get to where He needs them to be so that they can finish the race they now run with patience and diligence.

The children of the World cannot see the Kingdom of

God; therefore, the storm overtakes them and they fall. They fall and are subject to the storm and the storm determines how their life turns out. They have no control over the storm because they are out of relationship with God and have no hope of surviving it because they have chosen to trust in something other than His Word. The storm keeps them running in circles and they never get anywhere in life no matter what their accomplishments are or how much money they make. They are still stuck in the whirlwind of the storm; not realizing that the only way to experience true richest and wealth is to know Jesus. They give up their souls in the storm for temporary success and temporary wealth that will only last for a season.

They have no control over the storm because they are out of relationship with God and have no hope of surviving it because they have chosen to trust in something other than His Word.

Jesus asked a question in Mark 8:36, ***For what will it profit a man if he gains the whole world, and to loses his soul (Nkjv)?*** The answer to His question is there is no profit; there is actually a great loss, and the storm reveals what has been lost by the hopelessness it brings with it. The feeling of despair, void or having no reason for living is the midst of the storm that tackles the lives of those who are not children of the Kingdom of God. The constant press of loneliness and hatred toward yourself and fear reveals to you the storm in your life. Unless you give in and say I don't want to be a child of the World any more, I want to be a child of the Kingdom of God, then the storm will continue to overtake you. The children of the World are completely defeated against the storm of life, and the children of the Kingdom of God have already defeated the storm through the finished work of Jesus Christ. This happened when He proclaimed and pronounced on the cross that, "IT IS FINISHED." This pronouncement let the entire world know that Jesus alone has defeated the kingdom of this World, Jesus alone has taken away man's sin, Jesus alone has established His kingdom on the Earth and will continue to establish it through many sons in His Kingdom.

The storm is over for those in the Kingdom of God and they continue to remind it every time it tries to influence or dictate their life. They talk to it and proclaim to it the same words their king has proclaimed, "IT IS FINISHED." I am a child of God, and sin will not have dominion over me. They declare, I have overcome by the blood of the lamb and the word of my testimony (Revelation 12:11). The children of the Kingdom of God understand that they have complete authority over every storm that tries to come up against them and that no weapon formed against them shall prosper (Isaiah 54:17). They always triumph through Christ Jesus in every area of their life; THEY ARE CHAMPIONS.

2 Corinthians 2:14

Now thanks be to God who always leads us in triumph in Christ, and through us diffuses the fragrance of His knowledge in every place (Nkjv).

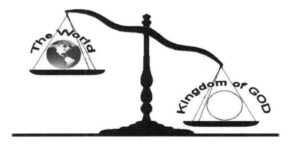

Chapter 9

God's Love

1 John 4:7, 8

Beloved, let us love one another, for love is of God; and everyone who loves is born of God and knows God. He who does not love does not know God, for God is love *(Nkjv)*.

The undeniable love of God is in itself the greatest force that man has ever encountered. It is the most gripping and fearful thing ever known. This makes all other competition fade and cease away without ever being able to come close. His love for man is so great, so intense and so aggressive that it makes man love Him back. *We love Him*, the Word of God says in 1 John 4:19, *because He first loved us*. It is His love that really makes all other things of lesser value worth nothing.

The revelation of His love brought His kingdom to men that they might experience His life. His life is in His son, Jesus Christ, the living and abiding Word of God. What no one could ever do, He made possible through His Son by expressing His love for man in Him. He sent His Son to take the place of everything we have done wrong, even all the way back to Adam in the garden. His Son gave us life by dying for our sins that condemned us to death. His Son brought us back into a covenant with God that no one can break. His love for us has made us at peace with Him and brought us back into an everlasting relationship with Him.

The part that many miss is that He only wants what is best for man. He loves man more than man can even comprehend. We must come to Him to see the love that only thinks good thoughts about us, the love that keeps His mind full of us, the love that embraces us as we are, the love that drives us to give our best and the love that causes us to love others. The World will never be able to compare to such a determined, strong and aggressive love that God has for us.

The world will never be able to compare to such a determined, strong and aggressive love that God has for us.

In His love, the World is forgiven and whoever desires to come to Him to enter into a relationship with Him can, through His Son Jesus. The Word of God says in John

3:16 *for God so LOVED the world that he gave his only begotten Son, that whosoever believe in him should not perish, but have everlasting life (Kjv).* His love for mankind is eternal; it is forever. He has made up His mind about man, and He is not changing it. He has already decided who man is, what man is like, how man lives and what man's future looks like in His Son Jesus, and it is final. There is no other kingdom strong enough to change or stop His decrees. He is the King of Kings, the maker of Heaven and Earth and of all that is in it. The smartest thing anyone can do is to agree with what He has said and accept His remarkable undeniable love for His own creation, man.

I was completely changed by His love, and I know that whoever He touches is forever changed. When He came to me for the first time, I didn't know or think that His love was what I came to find out that it is. I didn't even know this kind of love was possible until He begin to show me through His Word and our experiences together. It started when He asked me to lie before Him and I replied back, in my spirit, that it was a waste of time. I thought that it would be better for me to study the Word of God or pray than just to sit down quietly before God. Then the Holy Spirit spoke through a couple of people at my church to lie quietly before Him. I was finally obedient, and that is when I began to experience Him, and to hear from Him more than I ever heard from Him before. I began to spend more time with Him in order to get to know Him. There were many things He began to share with me as time went by, and I was obedient to what He told me to do. However, I made many mistakes during these times because of ignorance and at times, I did not want to get out of my comfort zone.

The Lord was always kind and loving, even in His strong authoritative voice that he used to rebuke me one time. I never felt so complete and filled with purpose. He made my life, as I trusted in Him, to be the most awesome and incredible life I could ever imagine. I have spent some very intimate, loving and glorious times with the Holy Spirit. We have laughed together; I have cried on His shoulder, and He has loved every bit of me the way that only He knows how. His words grip my whole being, and I am overwhelmed at His thoughts and plans for me. They are above and beyond all that I could have imagined on my own. He will not allow me to have anything less than all that He has promised, and He works diligently to make sure I walk in the reason for my existence.

There were some things that I just sensed would be the right thing to do, not knowing for sure with my mind but later, He would reveal to me that I made the right choice. In areas I didn't expect that He would be interested in, I was completely wrong. He was interested in everything and has a plan for every area of my life. He had already decided where He wanted me to go to school, where He wanted me to work, where He wanted me to go to church, where He wanted me to live, who He wanted me to be around and what he wanted me to do. He made plans way ahead of time before I was in my mother's womb how my life would be if I would follow His lead and enter into His kingdom. I thank God that when He chose me out of the World, He gave me the gift of faith to believe in Him, the grace to learn from Him, and His love to keep me, guide me and strengthen me in my walk with Him.

It was around two years after the Holy Spirit came, spoke to my heart and changed my life forever that I went back to school. I fought it because I didn't think that I was smart enough. I thought that it was a waste of time. However, God put a desire in my heart to go to school so that my ability to sing would match my unique God-given ability to write songs. This way I could write and sing my songs and bring out albums all over the world. Therefore, I enrolled in Marygrove College to study voice and to major in music. I ended up doing really well in music; I was practicing for hours daily on my vocals and piano skills. In my third or fourth semester, God opened a door for me to sing in an Opera. I never knew anything at all about Opera or classical music until I enrolled at Marygrove. If I wanted to become a trained singer, then that is what I had to learn, and I grew to like it a lot.

I went down with my teacher, Ms. Bigelow, to audition for Porgy & Bess at the Opera house in Detroit and I made the audition. There was no way that I could have made this kind of audition without the favor of God. They gave me a part in the chorus, and they put me in a lot of parts to act. It was one of those experiences that you will never forget, I really enjoyed performing. This happened all because my Father knew I would have fun performing; therefore, He made a way for me by opening a door for one more tenor to participate in Porgy & Bess. Many people have trained for years and years and have never performed in a live Opera like Porgy & Bess. This was one of His ways to express to me that if you delight yourself in Him, He will give you the desires of your heart (Psalms 37:4).

During my second year at Marygrove, I began to have strong desires jump up in my heart to take some business classes, not knowing why. All along, God knew exactly what He wanted me to do in life, and He was leading me and guiding me by His love for me. Therefore, I ended up changing my major to Accounting and making music my Minor. I did not know that God would allow me to do everything that I felt I had a gift for or was interested in until He begin to show me how much He had molded and made me for a specific purpose that involves the secular world as well as the church. He wanted me to see that He wanted me to press pass all limitations and grasp the reality of an abundant life that could not be measured by the World's achievements or accomplishments.

The call was higher than I imagined, and His love is far beyond my expectations. While I lay with Him in quietness, He continues to reveal to me my purpose and how He sees me. In His eyes, I am a champion; not going to one day become a champion, but I am a champion now. He treats me like a king and loves me better than a Father could ever love a son. Our relationship continues to grow as I allow Him to do whatever He desires in my life; which normally turns out to be the desires of my own heart. As I laid before Him, He allowed me to get to know Him and showed me things about myself that I didn't know.

The most incredible thing to me in our relationship was hearing from Him and feeling His presence. The things that He shared with me about my life were far beyond what I wanted for myself and far beyond what I could see. There were many things that I didn't understand at first, and then He would reveal them to me later. He always pushed me to strive and to give my best in whatever I did and helped me to stand in every circumstance that I had to face. The most beautiful thing about our relationship is that it seems like the worse things would get in my life, the more He would comfort me, strengthen me and keep me. My weakness was made perfect in His strength (2 Corinthians 12:9). When the enemy came in like a flood, the Spirit of the Lord would raise up a standard against him (Isaiah 59:19). I realize that I am the apple of His eye and because of that, He is the apple of my eye. I practice now keeping my mind stayed on Him throughout my day because I know that He is mindful of me. We share in the same love with one another, and I am forever His. Because of His love, I am forever changed.

I include the Holy Spirit in everything I do throughout my day; I am always talking to Him because He is my helper, my strength, my guide and my love. We have done so many things together, and He always forgives me when I make a mistake. Although I make mistakes, He is perfecting me. I still have a long way to go to be a complete reflection of my Lord Jesus, but I know that all things are possible to them that believe; therefore, I know that with His help, I will continue to press on and one day receive the prize. Nothing could ever be as amazing as our relationship. It is the best thing this world can offer, and it is the reason why I am able to write this book. I know that if nobody else in the world knows that the World cannot compare to the Kingdom of God, I Do!

Whenever I make a decision, He is always there to lead me and make sure I make the right choice. I am never alone, and He always comforts me when things happen that I take hard. I hate to offend Him, and when I do something that I know I should not have, it hurts me because of our relationship and the love that He has for me. His love is what changed me and what continues to make me a new person. I am only what Jesus Christ has made me because of His sacrifice, His unselfishness and His outpouring of love when He sent His Holy Spirit to live in me. With Him, I am complete and nothing can even come close to what it means to be complete in Him.

With Him added to my life, I have everything my heart and soul has ever truly desired. The deep parts of me that were covered by my flesh have only a taste for Him and His love brings my thirst and hunger for Him alive. I am completely undone by His love, and I believe once anyone truly comes to know His love, they will be completely undone as well. There is no way that you could know the love of Jesus and stay the same. You will be flooded with pureness and compassion until you are unable to be who you thought you were. His love is aggressive, yet gentle and filled with compassion and mercy, and it is wrapped in beauty and warmth. This touches the most sensitive places in man's being which brings man into his original state and position in Him.

There is no way that you could know the love of Jesus and stay the same

The Kingdom of God is real, and it is governed by a king that loves beyond what anyone could grasp on their own. It is because of our King Jesus that no other kingdom can compare. He is the Kingdom and His love upholds it and everything in it. The World could never come close; it will never be able to compare to the Kingdom of God. The World is only temporary and the things in it will not last much longer; however, the Kingdom of God will last forever and will never end. It is what makes life worth living, and it is the only thing that can give man hope. Without the Kingdom of God, the world will be without God's love; without God's love the world would be without LIFE.

1 John 4:4-6

You are of God, little children, and have overcome them, because He who is in you is greater than he who is in the world. They are of the world. Therefore they speak as of the world, and the world hears them. We are of God. He who knows God hears us; he who is not of God does not hear us. By this we know the spirit of truth and the spirit of error (Nkjv).

Reference

The New King James Version. Copyright 1979, 1980, 1982 by Arthur Farstad, Thomas Nelson Publishers, Nashville, Tennessee.

Prayer to enter the Kingdom of God

If you desire to be changed and to join God's unbeatable family, The Kingdom of God today and live a life lacking nothing, repeat this simple prayer out loud and mean it from your heart. Believe me, as you continue to pursue a personal relationship with the Lord Jesus Christ, you will be changed and see clearly that He is the supplier of all your needs. The Father's desire is that you come to Him believing and trusting that He is able to do what He promised you in His Word. That is to change you, make you a new person and to bring you into His family, The Kingdom of God. If you believe that Jesus can do that for you, say this prayer out loud and mean it from your heart.

Dear heavenly Father, I come to you today admitting that I am a sinner. Father, I ask you to forgive me for all my sins that I have committed against you and others. Father, I confess that Jesus is Lord and I make Him Lord over my life today and forever. I believe that Jesus died on the cross to take away my sins and I believe in my heart that on the third day, you raised Him from the dead. Father, I choose to turn away from my sins and to turn to you. I choose to trust in you with all of my heart and not to lean on my own understanding. Father, I choose to forgive every individual who has ever hurt me or who has ever done anything wrong to me. Father, I choose to forgive my biological mother and father. I choose to honor them and walk in love toward them that I might live a prosperous long life in the earth. Father, I choose to follow and obey your every Word and I ask that you fill me now with the power of your Holy Spirit. I declare and proclaim that right now, I am a child of God. I am completely free from sin and full of the righteousness of God. I declare that I am saved in Jesus name. Amen

If you repeated that prayer and meant it in your heart, you are no longer a sinner that is a part of Satan's family but you are now saved by God's grace and have entered into the

Kingdom of God. Rejoice and be glad! You are a new person. Now I encourage you to become a doer of the Word of God and not just a hearer, join a good church home that loves people and God and spend time each day talking to your heavenly Father. Remember, no matter what you are facing, He is always with you. He is your present help in the time of troubles. If your life has been changed or enriched by this book, visit us at AngelsMusicMMIX.com and share with us your testimony.

E. L. Brown is a humble, compassionate, courageous, and gifted young man after God's own heart. He has been called by God as a Seer and commissioned by God to take territory for the Kingdom of God. He graduated from MaryGrove College in 2009 with a Bachelors of Arts degree in accounting and a minor in music. He currently attends Wayne State University and is enrolled in their MBA program with an expectation to graduate in May, 2011. He was ordained a minister of the gospel of Jesus Christ in 2007 at New Breakthrough Church International under the leadership of Apostle Donald Coleman where he still resides. He was appointed as the youth director over NBCI youth department in 2008. He ministers weekly at Dickerson Prison, he's involved in street ministry, and he also has been called on by many churches to speak. Eric's desire is that every person experience God's love and that the Body of Christ will walk in oneness with God and with one another.

ANGEL'S MUSIC INC.
"Heaven's Delight"

Vision

<u>*That the whole world is filled with the sound from Heaven*</u>

ANGEL'S MUSIC INC.
"Heaven's Delight"

Follow E.L. Brown on twitter at
www.twitter.com/ELBrown2011 & on facebook at E.L.Brown

Go to our website and download our latest song, "**Abba Father**" for only 99 cents on your Iphone and find out what other products Angel's Music Inc. has for sale.

AngelsMusicMMIX.com

Thank you again for your purchase, may God bless you and keep you.